"If Emily Dickinson and Mark Twain had a child together, it wouldn't be Sean Vernon. Sean is no Emily Dickinson. He's much funnier, and he's a better storyteller. He's no Mark Twain either. He writes better poetry than Twain, and is far less ornery than Twain or anyone who smokes a cigar. I do know one thing for sure: If Emily Dickinson and Mark Twain could read Sean Vernon's memoir they would see themselves somewhere in it. I'm in it. You're in it. Anyone who is truly alive, or wants to be, will find every shadow and every sweet slant of light in Sean's life. We're lucky to share this earth with him and, in this book, to see it through his eyes."

~ Dan Lombardo, Author of *A Hedge Away, The Other Side of Emily Dickinson's Amherst*

ALL THE MEADOWS WIDE

a story of hope
and resilience

CROW FLIES PRESS
PO BOX 614 SOUTH EGREMONT, MA 01258 (413)-281-7015
www.crowfliespress.com
publisher@crowfliespress.com

Cover artwork by Tracy Vernon
tracyvernondesigns.com

Book design by Anna Myers

ALL THE MEADOWS WIDE

ISBN: 978-0-9983139-7-9
Copyright © 2025 Crow Flies Press
Printed in the USA

ALL THE MEADOWS WIDE

a story of hope
and resilience

SEAN VERNON

Crow Flies Press | South Egremont, Massachusetts

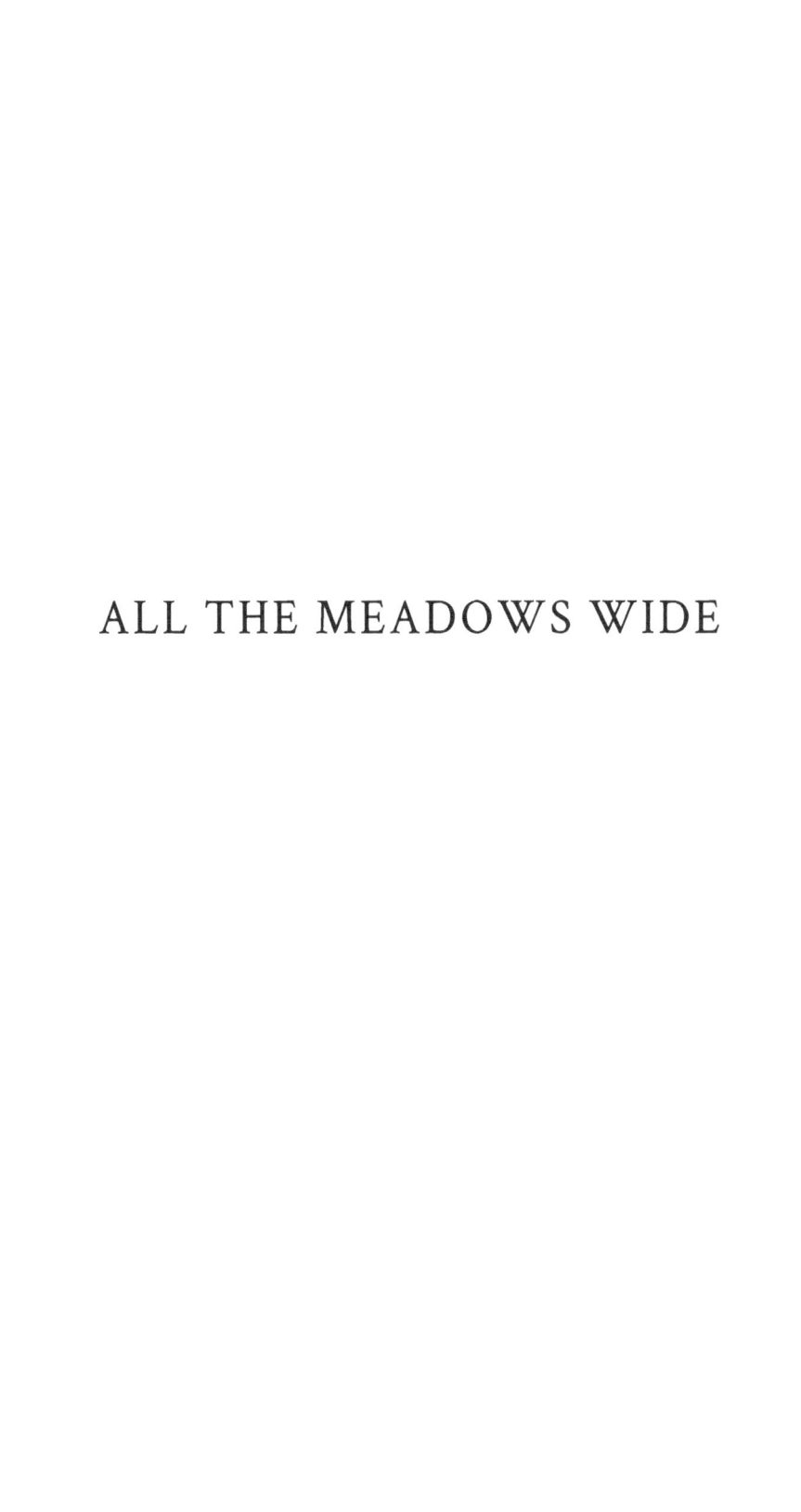

ALL THE MEADOWS WIDE

Also by Sean Vernon

Books:

Configurations

Blanket of Stars (co-author)

Albums:

Wider Than The Sky
(musical settings of poems by Emily Dickinson)

This and My Heart
(musical settings of poems by Emily Dickinson)

Four Williams
(musical settings of poems by Shakespeare, Yeats, Wordsworth, and Blake)

Acquainted With The Night
(musical settings of poems by Robert Frost)

Venus Unwound (original songs)

Walk Me Down (original songs)

Go Slowly Autumn (original songs & settings)

CONTENTS

CHAPTER 1
Unaffordable Housing............................1

CHAPTER 2
County Fair.......................................9

CHAPTER 3
The Sounds of Long Island......................15

CHAPTER 4
High School......................................26

CHAPTER 5
The Operation...................................35

CHAPTER 6
Jumping To Conclusions.........................40

CHAPTER 7
Down The Stairs.................................47

CHAPTER 8
Shakespeare in New Jersey......................57

CHAPTER 9
Third Floor......................................69

CHAPTER 10
In the Jungle............................73

CHAPTER 11
Iowa....................................77

CHAPTER 12
Denial is Not a River....................94

CHAPTER 13
Cinema.................................109

CHAPTER 14
Fall Risk..............................116

CHAPTER 15
Love Crimes............................132

CHAPTER 16
Surfacing..............................153

CHAPTER 17
Life In The Slow Lane..................170

Acknowledgments........................201

It's all I have to bring today—
This, and my heart beside—
This, and my heart, and all the fields—
And all the meadows wide—
Be sure you count—should I forget
Some one the sum could tell—
This, and my heart, and all the Bees
Which in the Clover dwell.

~ Emily Dickinson

To my brother

Prologue

This is the story about life with a debilitating disease. The title is pretty, thanks to Emily Dickinson, but the story is often not. If you want to learn about a life leading up to and coping with multiple sclerosis, or any disease, this book might be for you.

When I was a boy, fears of getting a serious illness took up very little space in my brain. I was prepared for brief run-ins with the standard childhood sicknesses—mumps, measles, chicken pox, but I didn't fret about anything more serious. A high caliber disease would soon have me in its crosshairs. I'd heard of Multiple Sclerosis, MS, but knew nothing about it. That would soon change.

What is MS? Imagine an electrical cord, with its insulating rubber worn away, frayed and in shreds, causing shorts in the wire, making it dangerous to touch, eventually shorting out the entire system. That's MS. The beautiful myelin sheath in my brain, my electrical cords, as it were, are frayed and misfiring, causing my nervous system, and in fact, my entire body to break down.

But, my life hasn't been all bad, so don't worry, it's not all gloom and doom. There's lots of humor and some poetry in this book. Even a bit of romance. The bottom line is, it's a memoir about my life with MS. And I've been dealing with it for more than forty years. But I'm still alive, still here, my mind is still working, even if my body is not. My heart still beats, my brain still creates, and I can still smell the flowers. I was in denial for most of my young adult life, but now, at sixty-eight years old, from my wheelchair, I'm living in a reality I wouldn't wish on anyone. And yet...

I decided on the title, ALL THE MEADOWS WIDE, because the poem felt like hope. Emily writes about hope a lot. And it's something I still have, despite everything.

Sean Vernon

CHAPTER 1

Unaffordable Housing

Arriving

I am a momentary mixture
of molecules and longing,
a man playing at blindness.
The truth weighs in all around me,
and I pretend not to see.
I am a dream,
a fading memory
of someone I never was.
My bones,
my teeth, which are bones,
my hands, which are bones grasping at dust,
is this the all of me?
Then why am I waiting for a blossoming world to find me again?
I want to return to my life with all its flaws—
I am busy making peace with each one.

I had to move. I was pretty sure I wouldn't much like living at the MacDougall House, the low-income apartment-complex a few towns away from where I'd been living for twenty years. I had driven past MacDougall many times and was always glad to see it drop out of sight in my rear-view mirror. The place made me a little sad for the people who lived there. But I could afford the rent there, a feature I couldn't ignore. The MS—which had proved uncooperative and demanding—had seen to it that my working full-time, especially at a job like teaching high school English, had become a memory after ten years. And MacDougall had elevators. This was a feature not lost on me, as walking more than a block had become a challenge. It joined a growing list of tasks I now needed help with, such as cooking, scrubbing the floor, showering, and tying my shoes. I had been able to reside places independently and very happily for many years. I took for granted that I would never need to relocate; especially to a place like this.

 The five-story brick building sat across town from a venerable liberal arts college housed on a lovely, tree-lined campus complete with a pond and wooded trails. I reminded myself that I'd have a roof over my head and be just down the hill from an attractive town with its restaurants, art galleries, and parks. I decided no better offers would likely be coming my way, so I decided to pay a visit and have a look around.

 At MacDougall, I spent my life among a cast of peculiar characters, like the man who strode down the hall and across the lawn on a high-flying ego, and who had somehow believed himself to be a monk, a spiritual light to everyone who lived there. There was a woman who locked herself in her apartment every day and made batches of crystal meth. A few doors away from her lived a man who blatantly cheated on his girlfriend with another one of the tenants. By some sort of reverse miracle, his girlfriend (unlike most everyone else in the building) didn't seem to notice. Directly below me, one floor down, was a woman who had regular shouting matches with her son (who was secretly living with her), an ex-marine who had apparently left pieces of his mind in Iraq. His mother, who I sometimes ran into in the laundry room, had rescued him from his life in the woods a few miles away. My closest neighbor, who occupied very cluttered rooms on the other side of my wall, was a sweet, intelligent woman who got drunk every night, hardly an unusual lifestyle choice for tenants in that building.

Pretty much everyone in MacDougall smoked, including most tenants and every member of the staff, including the director, the building manager, and the head of maintenance. People smoked on the benches outside the back door of the building, on their balconies, in the parking lot and, of course, in their apartments. I've never been a smoker, but I sometimes wondered how much second-hand smoke I was breathing in there and worried I would get lung cancer.

Across the hall from me at MacDougall lived Francie and Thomas. From their open door, I could see rickety furniture, piles of unwashed clothing, and scattered dirty dishes. And they smoked. Francie often told me she was about to quit, but her fingers remained discolored because of the nicotine. She was about 4'8" and almost as wide as she was long. Her hair was stiff and wiry, and because of her lazy eye, both eyes never looked in exactly the same direction. But I had been fond of her since the moment we met.

The first time I ran into her in the hallway, she told me about the brother she adored and had lost to MS. I don't think she knew my situation, but she must have had a hunch. I suspected her brother's condition had been more serious than mine. I wasn't anxious to hear any details, but I couldn't help asking her how the disease killed him.

"It didn't," she said. "Although, I guess it did. He committed suicide. He would never have done that if he'd been well."

I was stunned. Death had come a little too close.

In my eight years at MacDougall, I employed a series of PCAs—personal care attendants. Each of them would spend several hours a week with me and help with things that had become hard for me to do on my own. It always took me some time to find a reliable PCA. Some were always late, most left before their shift was over, the majority failed to do the things I asked them to do, and one stopped showing up at all. Take Cheryl, a middle-aged woman with kind eyes and a ready smile. On her first (and last) day, she took me shopping. I was headed to the cash registers to pay, when she turned to me.

"I have to be going," she said.

"OK," I returned. "This will only take a minute."

"I have to go," she said blankly. And she immediately turned and walked out the door. I never saw her again. I took a taxi home.

A man named Carl worked the late shift and would promptly go to sleep on my couch. After an hour or so I would wake him up and tell him to go home and get some sleep. The next afternoon when he came by, he greeted me warmly, sat down on the couch, and fell asleep again. Sherry was a slightly overweight born-again Christian who worked for me one summer. She was perpetually on a diet and was currently taking a risky weight loss formula full of amphetamines. This made Sherry work fast, talk fast and ultimately crash. Britt would come to my apartment reeking of marijuana and spent a lot of time on my veranda watching people pass by in the parking lot five floors below. Sherry was an attractive young woman who wore a very short skirt on her first (and last) day. During that one day, she sat across from me and slowly and seductively spread lotion on her thighs.

One of my last PCAs was a woman named April who had just left high school. She seemed to suffer from Munchausen by proxy, a syndrome that made her need me to be sick and play the role of her child. If I got what she considered too loud, she would tell me to use my "indoor voice." In the last month she worked for me, a friend of mine invited me to dinner and she drove me. I talked to this friend a few days later and thanked him for the meal and his company. He said he was glad he met April and was very glad when she left.

Early one beautiful July morning, I was on the bike path in my wheelchair, heading to the YMCA to swim. Swimming is something I've loved since I was a boy, though I've never been much of a swimmer. Just being in the water is enough for me. Weather permitting, I would go to the pool five or six times a week and spend an hour in the water. It was very therapeutic.

On the bike path I'd be surrounded by trees and grass and flowers. Every so often, a rabbit would hop out of the bushes and stand on the pavement looking around; then the creature would slip back into the darkness and continue doing what-ever rabbits do. I'd continue down the trail, waving to the people I passed, some of them pedaling along, others walking or running. Most of them seemed happy and smiled at me as they went by.

After a half hour, I'd cross the street and pull into the YMCA parking lot. I'd head up to the handicapped accessible front door, which I opened with a hand control fixed to the wall. I am very grateful for that device, as so few places have them. I've become unable to open lots of doors or even reach them. The word "access' didn't used to mean so much to me.

At the Y, I'd cruise through the lobby and enter the men's locker room. I would take off whatever I was wearing over my swim trunks and get back into my chair. It was one of my most challenging tasks of the day. I'd have showered before leaving home, so I went directly into the pool area. I'd wheel to the edge of the pool and call over one of the lifeguards for help getting into the pool-side chair. It would lower me slowly, and in a few seconds I'd be on my feet in the water. There was hardly a place I'd rather be.

For the next hour, I'd be perfectly content. I wouldn't do anything fancy in the water and didn't need to. I believe happiness is a simple formula. When I'm in the water, I look like anyone else. I don't require anything or anyone to help me get around. I can't use a walker in the pool and don't need to. I used to love taking long walks by myself; I journeyed for hours in the countryside, spent days combing the beach, kneeling on the sand to collect stones and shells. I stood on hilltops and took in the views all around me. I felt like a bird, untethered and free. Being in the water gave me that same feeling.

On my way home, people would pass me on the path; walking, running, or riding a bicycle. I smiled at some of them as they went by; few greeted me, but most said not a word.

One day, I was about to pass a man and his daughter who were walking up the path toward me from the other direction. As they approached, the girl looked at me and said hello with no trace of a need to put distance between us. She marched up to me without hesitation.

"What's that?" she asked me, pointing to the knob on my control panel.

"It's what makes it go," I answered.

"Can I try it?" she said, meeting my eyes. I knew enough not to say no. I looked at her father to make sure it was OK with him. He smiled at me and nodded.

"Sure," I said. "Come up on the seat." She climbed onto the chair and sat directly in front of me. In a few moments, she placed her tiny hand on the throttle and pushed it forward an inch. The chair lurched, almost running over her father's feet. He quickly stepped aside. I gently removed her hand, and the chair instantly stopped.

"We should probably turn the speed down," I said to her gently. "See this little window?" I asked, pointing to it. "It shows what gear you're in. The higher the gear, the faster you go. Right now, it's at five. That's the highest gear we've got. What do you say we lower it?"

"I guess so," she said. "Can I steer?"

"Sure," I said. I didn't really know what else I could have told her.

We rolled a few feet forward and stopped. She climbed off, beaming at her father who was beside us.

"That was great, honey," he said. He looked at me and smiled. "Thank you." The two of them started walking away and the girl turned to me for a moment and smiled. Then they were gone.

In the wee hours of the mornings, I'd often roll out of bed and get into my wheelchair. I'd take the elevator down five floors and slip away from the dirty white brick walls of MacDougall. I'd ease down the ramp into the parking lot, happy to be free of the cigarette smoke and the oppression of the building. I'd leave the parking lot and cruise slowly up the hill and through the center of town, seeing hardly a soul. In ten or fifteen minutes, I'd reach the college campus several blocks away; I'd explore the grounds on my solitary journey, cruising slowly past student housing, classroom buildings, the library with its dark windows and empty sidewalks, rolling slowly and silently along the empty shores of the campus pond. I would finally arrive at dead-end streets and ghost-like neighborhoods, feeling completely independent and alone, making no impression on the lives being lived all around me. Free to be soundless and invisible.

CHAPTER 2

County Fair

White Stallion

I lead a white stallion
beyond the fading sycamores,
as he nurses a fragile dream
of being set loose,
his mane flying free
like flames
scorching the earth
and sending up dust in smoky ribbons.
He eyes the distant hills
that are turning roe
in the still, evening light,
painting the moon and the stars
with the freedom of an untethered mind.
He will step away from the mission house,
and the ordinary,
cleaving the boundless
from the torture of routine.

**He will walk into himself,
resurrect life from the stony ground
and breathe.**

On a warm morning in June, I was slowly tumbling out of my dreams amid images of people streaming from a grassy field toward a row of silver turnstiles. Under bright blue tents stood concession stands brimming with cotton candy and bowls of vanilla ice cream with chocolate sprinkles. Suddenly, my six-year-old self passed through the fog of sleep and remembered that today was our annual trip to the county fair. After a quick breakfast, the twins, Christian and Claudia, and I climbed into the back of my father's Buick. My mother, several months pregnant, wearing her white and green checkered kerchief, sat comfortably in the passenger seat. In a few minutes my father arrived and slid into the driver's seat. My mother knew well what was coming: my father inserted the key into the ignition, buckled his seat belt, then after a moment's hesitation, unbuckled his seat belt, climbed out. My mother shook her head.

"Back in a minute," he said brightly and pointlessly before heading off to the house and his ordained rendezvous with the toilet. After sitting in the car for the better part of eternity, I joyously watched my father once again emerge from the house, whistling. He was now ready to begin driving to the fairgrounds on the Pennsylvania border roughly an hour west. For me, going to the fair was on par with watching the Fourth of July fireworks from the second-floor porch outside my sister's bedroom.

For the next hour, I sat against the window, watching the world fly past. We rolled through farmland, climbing long, gentle slopes and coasting down the other side. Finally, we reached the final leg of our trip. From the top of a hill, we looked down and saw the fairgrounds with their churning crowds and swarming food courts. In a few minutes, we were pulling in and scouting for a parking place. After buying our tickets and walking ahead with the other visitors, we split up; Claudia and my mother decided to follow the signs for the animal showcases and the handling areas. They were eager to tour the monkey house, give crackers to the goats and spend some time with the llamas. Claudia spent the most time with the llamas, thrilled to be so close to the big, gentle creatures.

My father walked with Christian and me as we passed the lines for the various rides. "There's one I want you to see," he said, pointing ahead and looking up. "It's called The Slide."

Christian and I also looked at it.

"Are you guys interested in trying it?"

"I am," said Christian.

"Definitely," I answered.

"Let's go then," said my father, and he led us down the path. He guided us past the Tilt-a-Whirl, Roller Coaster, and the Ferris Wheel. In a few minutes, we reached our destination. The Slide was the tallest thing I'd ever seen. My brother and I looked at my dad, who nodded in acknowledgment, urging us to start the climb to the top. We began our ascent and the higher we climbed, the more I was regretting my decision. A man in overalls was standing at the top.

"This way, boys," he said. He held out a mat to each of us. "You're going to ride these to the bottom," he said. I turned my head and looked for a moment over the fairgrounds. Beyond the rides and the stands of games and stuffed animals, potato salad and ears of corn, crowds of people were milling about, eating and talking. I looked past the parking lot and saw a line of trees beneath the dark green hills. Suddenly, I felt a little queasy.

"Are you sure you want to do this?" I asked Christian softly.

"Don't tell me you're turning chicken!" Christian scoffed at me with a grin. "What *are* you, a girl? Why don't you pet the bunnies?"

"I was only saying," I shot back. "Maybe it's a terrible ride."

"You don't have to go," he said. "I'll meet you at the bottom."

The man looked at Christian. "You his older brother?" he asked him. Christian nodded. "OK, you go first, then. Show your brother how it's done."

Christian immediately stepped forward and dropped his mat. "Follow me, if you dare," he said, looking at me and laughing. A moment later, he was gone. I moved up quickly, got onto my mat, and followed him down. As the wind whipped back my hair and whistled past my ears, I knew I had made a mistake. It seemed possible I could tip my mat over the edge of the track and plummet to an early death. I promptly sat up and focused on keeping my balance. My stomach started to flutter and didn't settle down until I came to a sudden stop in the grass. My brother was standing there grinning at me. He reached out a hand and pulled me to my feet.

"How'd you like that, boys?" my father greeted us.

"It was great," I said, telling my father what he wanted to hear.

"How about a few more rides?" he said, handing us each some tickets.

My brother gladly took them, and led me over to the Tilt-A-Whirl. Watching the people staggering off the ride, I could already feel my stomach starting to groan.

On our way out of the fairgrounds, we came upon a man selling helium balloons.

"You guys should each get a balloon," my mother suggested. Claudia shook her head. "I don't want one," she said. "I'd much rather have my own llama."

Christian looked at her. "What are you going to do with a llama? Take it for walks around the neighborhood? Where's it going to sleep? At the foot of your bed?"

"You're such an idiot," she told him.

"What about you?" my mother asked me. "You want a balloon?"

"Definitely," I said.

"What color do you want?"

I looked them over. "The green one!" I answered, quickly.

"That was fast!" said my father. "Look at them all."

"I want the green one," I said. I didn't need to think it over. It seemed to me that my father thought I was making a mistake, but I didn't care. Green was my favorite color. It was the color of spring.

My father stepped up, paid for the balloon, and handed me the string. I instantly wrapped it around my wrist.

Once we were all settled in the car, my father turned the key in the ignition. I was sad to be leaving the fairgrounds but happy to be holding the green balloon. It was rolling back and forth against the ceiling, and I watched it steadily. I wanted to protect it from sharp things. The balloon had known nothing but upward mobility in its short life. It would never stop ascending and would be limited only by ceilings and pieces of string.

No one said much on the way home. Eventually, we pulled into our driveway, each of us a little worn out from our day at the fairgrounds. I carried the balloon out of the car and stood in the driveway. I hadn't won the balloon, but it still felt like a prize. It was mine, and I wasn't about to let anyone get too close to it.

"What's with you and that stupid thing," Christian asked as he passed.

"Jealous?" I responded. "You just wish *you* had one."

"I sure *don't*," he shot back. "I've got much better things to do with my time. Don't let it pop!" he said, shaking his head as he walked to the back door.

For no good reason, I began playing a game that was sure to end badly. I would untie the balloon and let it float away for a second or two, then I'd catch the string and pull the balloon back down. One time I let it rise a second too long, and when I reached for the string, it eluded my grasp. Suddenly panicked, I watched the balloon escaping. In a moment, it began to sail above the kitchen window. My father passed behind me, and I whirled around.

"Dad, get the ladder!" I cried. "Grab the string!" I gestured at the rapidly departing balloon.

My father looked up at the balloon and turned to me. "It's no use, Buddy," he said gently, putting a hand on my shoulder. "That one's not coming back. Don't worry, I'll get you another one tomorrow." He disappeared into the house.

But I didn't want another one. I wanted that one. I watched the green balloon sail over the roof and slowly disappear. Afraid my brother might come out of the house and poke fun at me for being upset, I quickly retreated to the backyard and lay down in the grass. I placed my hands over my eyes and tried not to think. I could feel the grass becoming a little damp and the air heating up in the summer afternoon. I closed my eyes and tried to turn off my brain. "Stupid balloon," I whispered to myself.

CHAPTER 3

The Sounds of Long Island

Liquid Evening

This liquid evening
showers its fragrant bouquet
of wild tendrils reaching for love
across bluing dirt,
like misty skin,
like honey'd blood.
The wind mispronounces its own name,
The vein-crossed leaves
drop like paper bombs
to the waiting ground in ultimate surrender.
Not one angel cries out
not one soul is bruised,
and no stone speaks of regret.

My father grew roses. Some days, I'd stand at the edge of the garden and watch him sprinkle fertilizer on the soil. Then he usually lay down a hose and let the water seep to the roots. Many times, in the summer and early fall, he clipped a few roses and set them in vases on the kitchen counter and the dining room table. I suppose I wanted him to be as proud of me as he was of those flowers, and I usually thought I was holding my own.

But, one time I felt myself plummet from grace in my father's eyes. When I was ten, my father connected a basketball hoop to a piece of plywood the size and shape of a standard backboard. He nailed it ten feet off the ground into a small pine tree at the edge of our driveway. I spent many happy hours under the basket, playing entire games in my head and on the "court." My favorite player, the best one in the entire league, bore a striking resemblance to me. I always placed my mother's kitchen timer on the ground beside the tree and kept each game to about half an hour long. My team had to win every game, preferably in the last few seconds: I loved dramatic finishes! To make for a breathtaking (and satisfying) last few seconds, I had to sink the final shot. This day, as usual, I ran up to the basket and lofted the ball with only moments left on the clock. I had sunk the shot countless times; this was wasn't one of them.

"God dammit!" I screamed when the ball struck the rim and fell to the ground. I'd forgotten my father had installed an intercom system throughout the house and had attached one of the microphones to the shutter beside the front door. The speaker allowed someone in the house to hear things happening outside.

"Get in here this minute!" my father thundered through the tiny grill, as though God himself were addressing me. I froze. I dropped the basketball, raced through the front door and up the stairs to my room. I threw myself on the bed, buried my face in the pillow and started to cry. It was one thing to condemn my own failures but far worse to get reprimanded by God himself.

We were off to the tip of Long Island the next day to visit Nanny, my father's mother. Christian and Claudia, my brother and sister, looked forward to this annual trip as much as I did, more than anything we did all year—with the possible exception of celebrating Christmas. I was terrified the trip to Long Island would be canceled by my temper tantrum. But to my immense relief, my outburst was not a gamechanger. I guess I didn't wield that much power after all.

*

For the last 40 years of her life, Nanny, my father's mother, lived in Greenport, Long Island, once a quiet, impoverished town on the north fork. Greenport came to life in the summer, when Preston's Marina filled with sailboats and the occasional cabin cruiser. Summer residents lined the decks of the Shelter Island ferries that plied the waters of Gardiner's Bay several times an hour. Afternoons were long and sleepy and punctuated by low blasts from the bunker boats that worked the Atlantic for a silvery fish called menhaden.

Nanny had grown up in New York City, with a hundred pairs of shoes in her closet and a limousine waiting at the curb on school mornings. But she married a handsome man of immense charm who had trouble turning down a drink. 'Gramps,' my father's father, partied and gambled Nanny out of all the money her parents had left her. Forced to work for the first time in her life, she took a job as a secretary at *Time Magazine* in Manhattan, filing for divorce at a time when it was far less common than it is today. She assumed the task of raising two children on her own, one of them my father.

For the few years I knew him, Gramps was an empty shell of a man. I don't even remember the sound of his voice. Gramps shared a few of our Thanksgiving meals, though he never spent the night, probably because my father hadn't invited him to stay. My father always made sure Nanny and Gramps sat on opposite sides of the table. They spoke to each other a few times during the meal, but only in short sentences that carried no hint of emotion and didn't touch on the past. Gramps wasn't really part of our family, so I never understood why he was there. I suppose my father felt obligated. And Nanny may have seen inviting Gramps over for holiday meals the kind and proper thing to do.

The sky started to brighten by the time we reached New York City an hour and a half after pulling out of our driveway. The sidewalks were virtually empty and most of the windows in the office buildings still dark. We soon left Manhattan and hopped on The Long Island Expressway. Every shadow had begun to lighten, and the number of cars we passed began to climb. Soon, the road became two lanes, and the water began to close in on both sides, Great Peconic Bay to the north, the Long Island Sound on the other side: to me, the Sound had always been a magical body of water, rich blue in the day, a dark, brooding, star-flecked channel at night.

I sat in the front seat between my mother and father and took in the sights flying past my window. Soon one of the lanes started peeling away, and my father turned to me and asked the magical question: "Do you want to steer for a while?" It was easily one of my favorite parts of the trip. Claudia always looked a little queasy at this inevitable development, but she never said a word. Riding in a car always made her a little nauseous, but when I began to steer, her discomfort bumped up a bit. Sometimes the road got a little rough, and my father put his hands beside mine until the surface smoothed. I turned unhappy for a moment but secretly glad that my father's big hands were on the wheel once again.

In a little while, we began to spot important landmarks and could tell we were getting close to the promised land. We whizzed by the miniature golf course, the bowling alley, the penny-candy store with its nonpareils and chunks of peanut butter fudge. Small blocks of commercialism gave way to stretches of roadway and the ever-trusty farmstands, with their tomatoes, cucumbers, potatoes, zucchini, radishes, ears of corn, and other important vestiges of summer. Finally, we were slowly cruising down Main Street in Greenport and soon drew up to the old age home, where residents rocked in unison on the front porch. Twenty yards down stood the towering furniture warehouse with its gables and cracked fourth story windows. Through them, every evening at dusk, a line of bats rose against the lavender sky. In the center of town, languid men and women sat on cane stools at the veranda of Claudio's restaurant. Down the block, an ancient movie theatre advertised films not many people had seen when they came out two years earlier. Perched on the wooden pilings beside the docks, seagulls paid close attention to people walking along the docks beneath them.

My father turned the car into Nanny's street, happy to have arrived. He felt drawn to the town for many reasons, the most important being his mother's presence. I never felt our visits lasted long enough, and I wasn't the only one who felt that way. My father drove past the chain link fence and pulled up the driveway, which rose slightly at the end, bringing us up to the garage doors. Nanny heard our car doors slam and came quickly down the wooden staircase. On reaching the bottom, she flung open the screen door and stepped lightly onto the porch. Bounding onto the stoop, she beamed at us.

"You made it!" she exclaimed. "I'm awfully glad!" When we all climbed out of the car, Nanny walked over and bent down. "Was that a terribly long ride?" she asked us needlessly. She knew it had been. Nanny would never have admitted it, not even to herself, but she couldn't help feeling flattered. "Let's go upstairs," she invited the group, clapping her hands. "Can I give you a hand?" she asked my father, seeing him pick up several boxes.

"Don't be silly," he said. "We've got it under control. You guys all head upstairs."

"Come on then!" Nanny said to us. We climbed the stairs and walked into the kitchen. We all breathed in the aroma of allspice, cinnamon, and ginger, ingredients that seasoned the delicious cookies, breads, and cakes she'd baked in her antique oven.

I headed into the living room by myself and walked through the doorway onto the glassed-in porch. Below me, the lawn stretched to a concrete wall rising four feet above a narrow beach. Nanny loved to sit on the sand and watch the small waves fold over quietly on the sand. Sometimes, she observed the horseshoe crabs sluggishly dragging themselves along. She loved to study them; it reminded her how grateful she was that her days of hurrying everywhere were done. To the left stood the small dock with a few small boats rocking in the shade. The slender wooden posts were bleached by the sun and covered in white barnacles.

Working together that night, Nanny and my mother turned out a delicious dinner of black bean stew, onion rings, and artichokes. We ran each leaf through a bowl of melted butter and with our teeth scraped off the succulent pulp.

After the meal, my father looked at us. "Hey, why don't you guys go down to the beach. I want to know if the tide's coming in or going out."

"How do we tell?" I asked him.

"Come on!" said Christian. "We can figure it out."

"That might take a few hours," I said, scornfully.

"Gee, do you think you can spare the time?" Christian asked me. "You got a big date or something?"

When Christian, Claudia and I reached the end of the lawn, Claudia turned to us, "See that little rowboat beside the dock? Do you think it belongs to anybody?"

"Of course, it belongs to somebody!" said Christian. "What, do you think, it just appeared there by magic?"

"I've never seen anyone around." Claudia said. "I sat out here a lot last summer. Nobody came by. Why couldn't we just borrow it? It wouldn't be stealing."

"I don't know," I said. "Dad would kill us."

"We'll just be gone ten minutes," said Claudia. "Who would even know?"

I thought about it for several seconds. "OK," I said, still not sure if it was a smart thing to do. "I guess I'll go."

"I'm rowing!" said Christian.

After looking around the area and finding no one about, we scrambled down the ladder and stepped into the boat. Christian slid the oars into the locks and we started to float away. The three of us looked across the surface of the bay, excited to feel that we were on our own. Sort of. We happily drank in the smell of salt water.

"I've got an idea!" said Claudia excitedly. "Let's go out to the jetty. I've always wanted to see it up close. Who knows what's out there?"

"All you'd find out there are rocks," I assured her.

"Yeah, and maybe some bird poop," said Christian.

"Plus, it's like a million miles away," I said.

Just then someone started yelling at us from the far side of the dock.

"What the hell are you brats doing in my boat!" a man shouted. "Bring it back this instant!"

Christian immediately turned the boat around and started rowing hard for shore. I looked ahead to see what the man was doing. Claudia covered her mouth and laughed quietly to herself. I heard her and smiled. She had just risen several notches in my estimation.

*

"Have you ever seen the shell of a horseshoe crab?" Nanny asked me one day, as we sat together on her beach.

"There was one here last time," I told her. "He must have gone home."

"Or she," Nanny said.

"Where do they live, anyway?"

"Some of them live right here in the bay," she answered. "There was a really big horseshoe crab shell down this beach a ways. I wonder if it's still there."

"Well, if it's not, I'm sure there'll be another one there soon enough," I said.

"We can learn a few things from them," Nanny said "Like how to survive in a world that's not always all that friendly. When you get older, you'll find out how dangerous this crazy world can be," she said. "It can take time and a little practice, but we learn how to survive it all, just like the horseshoe crab!" She was silent for a while. "Oh! I didn't tell you the most impressive thing about horseshoe crabs! They've been here since before the dinosaurs!"

"That's insane!" I cried. "They've been here for...like a million years! I'm sure not going to be here that long."

"You don't think so?"

"It's definitely a long shot," I said.

Nanny looked at me and smiled. "I love it when you guys are here," she said. "Can I say that?" She was quiet for a moment. "I guess I can. I think I just did." She looked at me for a long moment.

"OK," Nanny said. "You know, if we look around, we might find a moonstone or two. Let's see how many we can bump into right around us. They bring good luck, you know."

"I kind of doubt that." I said. "They're just rocks."

"They're as old as the sun," said Nanny. "That should be worth something, don't you think?"

To me, Nanny was worth a lot. Spending time with her was worth even more. I loved swimming with her in the gentle waters of the Sound, and walking alongside her searching for colorful seashells, beach glass, and braided pieces of driftwood. She never tired of taking strolls along the beaches, accompanied by calls of the gulls. I admired Nanny's energy, self-reliance, and refusal to be intimidated by people or events. Or by growing older. Once, she drove me and my father downtown in her white, two-door Rambler. After a few minutes in her car, Nanny at the wheel, my father was a little shaken. He declared her the only eighty-year-old in America who peeled out from a red light. She was gliding along in her final lap, but she didn't slow down. I very much doubt the idea ever crossed her mind. When I was in her company, I felt nothing could go seriously wrong in my world. But I never spent enough time with her, none of us did. She could only handle us for short visits. At the time, I didn't understand what a loner she was. And how much her privacy and independence meant to her. The day she died, I began to understand.

I loved my grandmother. She and my mother were both named "Helen," and each of them had a hard time letting people get close. A phone call to Nanny disappeared into a dial tone before the conversation had really begun. Even when the distance between us was no more than the width of her kitchen table, the gap didn't narrow.

I think in Nanny's view, life could not be trusted. She had probably eyed it doubtfully since the collapse of her marriage. I think she stood vigil against heartbreak, which might be waiting for her around the bend. Nanny's guerrilla-like stance probably served her well through most of her life, but in the end, the walls she had built to keep danger out, might have kept her locked in. Religion didn't seem to have figured a lot in her life. She must have decided it was a comfortable trap she needed to avoid in order to remain in control of her life. I've wondered whether, at the end of her life, she sensed the extent of her self-created isolation. Her staunch independence could well have undermined her ability to submit to something higher. Nanny may have lived as an outlaw too long to immediately turn herself in. She needed more time than she had.

In the church garden after Nanny's funeral, her friend Lisa told me about being there at the end of Nanny's life. One day, Nanny called Lisa and asked her if she could come by and keep her company. She said she was in some pain and feeling lonely. Lisa became concerned. Nanny had never shown any interest in going to church. When Nanny asked Lisa if she would bring along her Bible, Lisa became alarmed. She got on the next ferry to Greenport.

Half an hour later, Lisa was sitting on Nanny's bed. Lisa said Nanny looked shrunken against the clean, white pillowcase. Nanny had taken Lisa's hand, and, in a shaking voice, told her she felt close to dying and was very afraid. She asked Lisa if it was too late for her to become a Christian. Lisa said faith can come at any moment. Nanny asked Lisa to read something from the New Testament that might help calm her. With her free hand, Lisa opened to a familiar passage and began to read: "For God so loved the world that he gave his only begotten Son, that whosoever believed in Him should not perish, but have everlasting life."

Lisa read as the sky turned purple, and the bats, like a great moving shadow, swept out of the furniture warehouse down the street and flitted above the trees. Nanny had listened closely; strangely attentive for a woman of her restless nature. A little past nine, Nanny told Lisa she wanted to sleep. She thanked her very much for coming and sent Lisa home, making her promise to get some sleep herself.

Late that night the bunker boats streamed home from the black Atlantic, bellowing news of their return across the waters off Gardiner's Bay. Their foggy baritone voices rumbled down the Shelter Island shore, a sound Nanny had always heard as meaning all was well with the world. She felt herself being carried off by some irresistible tide toward the blackest sea of all.

Sometime around one o'clock in the morning, Nanny's heart stopped beating. In her last hours, Nanny made for a port she'd never visited, where the wind held words that came to her in murmurs, like a conversation across the waters of Gardiner's Bay.

CHAPTER 4

High School

Willow

A happy willow
stands on the fringe of the meadow
on a cloud-scattered day,
offering rest to weary birds
and shade against the flames of summer.
A playful, mindless breeze
encourages any branch that will listen
to sway without crying
giving lie to the name,
in a beautiful dishonesty.
The willow holds onto its leaves
long after the boughs of its neighbors have let go:
it always makes me smile
though I'm told I should weep.

I preferred high school to any of the grades below it. But not by much. In every grade, from kindergarten on, school felt to me like a prison. In my first year as a sophomore in high school, I started feeling that I badly needed an alternate route to graduation. Riding the school bus one morning in May, I started thinking about what classes I most wanted to skip. I realized it was pretty much all of them.

I considered where to begin and ran down the list. Algebra came to mind immediately. I didn't understand math very well, in general, and algebra hardly at all. I couldn't imagine ever using it outside the classroom. But there was a problem: Jennifer Bates. If I pulled the plug on algebra, I would probably lose any chance of winning her heart; or at least getting her to notice me. Still, I told myself to get real: Jennifer Bates was clearly out of my league. The problem was, she sat three seats down the row from me, and I liked her. A lot. Her presence made the room a good place to be for an hour; even if I was hopelessly confused by the symbols staring at me from the blackboard.

Then, there was earth science, mostly because the sound of Miss Ollom's nasally southern drawl made me squirm. I felt that if she ever had anything worth saying, her voice wouldn't have mattered that much.

I knew a student's absence from class was always reported and that a written notice would probably end up on the desk of Mr. Roberts, the Dean of boys. But I didn't know exactly what detention entailed, and I wanted to find out. In homeroom, one day, I turned to my neighbor, Norman.

"You've been in detention once or twice, haven't you?" I asked him.

"Yeah, so?" said Norman.

"I was just wondering what it's like."

"What it's like? You sit there for an hour and don't talk."

"Can you ask to see a lawyer?" Norman didn't even smile; for him, detention must not have been a laughing matter.

The dreaded earth science occupied third period for me, running from 10:00 to 11:05, so I had to find somewhere to hide for about an hour each morning. I thought of the auditorium and that it would be easy to hole up in the shadows backstage. For the most part, nobody really used the space much unless there was rehearsal, so, following geography with Miss Fletcher, I walked to the wing reserved for theatre arts. I quietly entered the deserted auditorium and climbed the short flight of stairs at the side of the stage. Once there, I looked around for a dark corner to pass a quiet hour. I spotted a wooden ladder attached to a backstage wall and leading up to a small space under the rafters. Confident I had found the ideal hideaway, I stepped onto the ladder and rose rung by rung to the top. I looked over and saw a small space perfectly suited to my needs. A little table stood there with a blue, wooden chair beside it.

I swung over and stepped onto the floor. I sat in the chair and ran my hands over the table top. I could imagine laying a book on it and disappearing into the pages. The prospect lifted my spirits immeasurably. I looked over the stage and the rows of seats, feeling myself floating above the entire scene. I couldn't imagine leaving this lofty perch and returning to those classroom-shaped coffins beneath me. I quickly came to believe that if skipping one class would preserve my sanity, I might well feel like a new man by skipping a bunch of them. Just by thinking about following through on this, I could feel life running through my veins again.

Lying in my bed that night, I added French to the growing list of classes I'd very much like not to be attending any longer. "Quel dommage!" (what a pity!) I could hear Mrs. Black (Madame Noir) say, if she learned I would no longer be in class. But really, how could that rank as a pity? It wouldn't be a pity to me, or to the school, probably not even to Mrs. Black. And I definitely wouldn't miss her horrid denim pant suits. Before I drifted off to sleep, Algebra came into my sights. I had already begun adopting a new identity, that of a suburban New Jersey Phantom of the Opera.

I soon realized the safest approach might be to never attend classes at all, to basically disappear. Being repeatedly caught skipping a few classes might make it hard for me to keep coming up with plausible explanations: *My house caught fire. I had to see a neurologist because of mysterious, extraordinarily painful headaches. My dog (I didn't own a dog) had been run over by an ambulance and was fighting for his life.* I chose not to try the patience of the high school staff, particularly Mr. Roberts. Instead, I turned fugitive, taking the school bus in every day but never showing my face in the classroom.

To me, Mr. Roberts was a dangerously unpredictable figure of authority. This man didn't care about the state of a student's mind—specifically mine. I had never talked to Mr. Roberts, but the man made me uneasy. Surely, I had made some bad mistake and would soon feel the sting of Roberts' lash. What my mistake might be, and what price I would pay for it, were unknown, maybe unknowable. This characterized many of the things that dwelled completely in my mind, where the reasonable light of day was sometimes absent. Most of my classmates talked about Mr. Roberts in hushed tones, as though he might be waiting for them around the corner. The girls had their own marshal,

Mrs. Andrus, Dean of girls. But she always tried to look the villain and so couldn't be taken all that seriously. But to me, Mr. Roberts was a different animal. He seemed friendly enough, but I never let down my guard around him. Such was the approach of almost every freshmen boy.

By the time June rolled around, I had skipped an entire week of classes and become comfortable in the role of school renegade; I liked to think I ranked as public enemy number one with Mr. Roberts. Though, at first, he had no hard proof of my presence on school grounds, I was sure he sensed me there. From time to time, he probably received accounts of me flitting down one of the school corridors or escaping out the front doors, but Mr. Roberts had almost certainly never spotted me on school grounds. The ghostly, labyrinthine world of the backstage proved a difficult place to corner a fast-moving wraith. Mr. Roberts lived in the world of fluorescent light; I was at home in shadows. One day, he came through the stage door from the well-lit hallway to have a look around. He was momentarily blind, and a moment was all I needed to draw back into the blackness. In my mind, catching me had become an important pursuit for Mr. Roberts.

One day he walked into the drama room where I was writing a story in my notebook. He marched up without a word, put a hand on my collar, and marched me down to his office. He made me sit at a desk and take four final exams in a row, not allowing me so much as a trip to the bathroom. I didn't mind at all. Like any notorious criminal I felt important. Mr. Roberts sat in the room with me the whole two hours, and he kept an eye on me, expecting me to choose my moment and bolt to the hallway. But I never stirred.

So, I started early in my career as a ghost, haunting out-of-the-way places, remaining largely invisible, spying on the living, who never suspected I was there. What had made a ghost of me? Mr. Roberts had given me a clue. An unacknowledged bond had formed between us: we were playing a game together, an elaborate type of hide and seek; the sound of his voice set my palms sweating, but my fear was mingled with excitement. I didn't take to the shadows simply to avoid Roberts: if I'd only wanted that, I would have played hooky the normal way and retreated far from the school grounds. I'd have piled into a car with two or three other guys and driven down to Asbury Park or Point Pleasant, spending the afternoon watching girls and playing skeeball in the boardwalk arcades. But I didn't have two or three friends to do that with, didn't even have one friend who was sufficiently adventurous. I played hooky in Roberts' front yard to invite pursuit. I felt as though he was the only person who cared enough to try to find me.

My parents didn't want me flunk out of high school—I may well have been on the edge of accomplishing it—so, at the end of that summer, they sat down with Mr. Roberts and told him their plan: they would ship me off to a private school for a year and hope it would help me see things differently. Going on the advice of the high school guidance counselor, they enrolled me in a private, Catholic prep school run by Benedictine monks.

Some of the students lived at school—others, like me commuted from home. To get to school, I rode a bus for half an hour every morning. At noon, I would hide out in the library and read a book eating the lunch my mother had packed for me. After my afternoon classes, I sat in the library for an hour and a half doing my homework and nothing else. All I wanted was to be left alone and do my work.

I hardly said a word to anyone the first month I was there. One day in October, I was befriended by a boy named Lee, a strong contender for least popular boy in school. I spent time in the library with him, poring over the latest boating magazines. I sometimes helped him pick out a yacht his father had promised to buy for him if he graduated in the top tenth of his class. I helped Lee with his English and geometry, and in return he promised to take me with him to Hawaii the following summer. I later discovered that he was at the school on scholarship—his father drove a cab in Irvington.

Every Monday before classes, convocation was held in the chapel. The dean would announce upcoming events and give a brief pep talk, encouraging students to always do their best and giving them words of inspiration to improve the chances of succeeding in school and all other parts of their lives. Nothing of those talks stayed with me for more than a few minutes. Attendance at convocation was mandatory; unexcused absences from it or any class brought a boy ten demerits. The discipline at the school was strict, and parents were immediately notified if their son received a demerit. If a boy received 30 of them, he was suspended for a week. At 40 demerits, a student was sent packing.

One Monday, I decided to risk being given ten demerits by hiding out in the library during convocation to read the last fifteen pages of *One Day In The Life Of Ivan Denisovich*, a novel by Alexander Solzhenitsyn we were supposed to have read before school that day. I just needed ten minutes to finish, so I decided to skip convocation and spend the hour in the library, finishing the book. At the rear of the library was a short corridor housing a row of carrels, tiny study rooms, about four square feet, that contained a shelf attached to the wall, a lamp, and a chair.

Ten minutes before the bell sounded, telling us to go to the chapel, I left my seat in the library and drifted back through the stacks, pretending to be browsing the shelves. Then I slipped into the dim corridor and hurried down to the last carrel in the row. I sat down, pulling the door closed behind me, and began to read. Within minutes I was frozen and starving, longing for gruel and a crust of bread. Because of the Siberian wind howling around me, I didn't hear the footsteps at first. But they came closer, and the spell cast by the novel disappeared—Siberia to New Jersey in a split second. I switched off the lamp, sat still, and listened. A few moments later, the door at the other end of the corridor creaked open, and someone started walking in my direction. I slid off the chair and crouched under the shelf in the darkness. I didn't think someone looking through the window could see me, but the steps came ever closer, so I retreated noiselessly over the floor and pressed myself against the wall.

The door opened, and a shadow entered the room. A moment later, the light on the shelf snapped on. I felt the shelf shudder as the person set down something heavy. An arm's length away, stood two trouser legs and a pair of brown Wingtip shoes. Aside from my father, the only person I'd ever seen in that style shoe was Mr. Murray, my French teacher. He sat down, and I heard him open a book. I was holding myself perpendicular to him, the left side of my body glued to the wall, my heart pounding. Three inches separated my leg and the toe of his left shoe. He sat with his knees bent, his feet flat on the floor. I could see that if he stretched his legs, I was finished. I had no place to go. All I could do was wait, and I didn't think the wait would be very long.

In a few seconds, Mr. Murray shifted again, and this time it was the slouch I'd feared. His shoe touched something solid yet soft, something that shouldn't have been there. With a start, he pushed back his chair and craned his neck down for a look. I'd never seen a person more surprised. He stood up, opened the door, and slipped into the hall. I instantly crawled out from under the shelf and followed him into the hall. Too embarrassed to look at him, I just stood next to the door, never taking my eyes off those Wingtips.

Neither of us spoke for a moment, then Mr. Murray, fighting down a chuckle, said, "I've heard of skipping convocation, but this is ridiculous!" There was nothing like anger in his voice—only astonishment. I nodded, mumbled some stab at an apology, and started down the hall. I assumed he would follow me out and take me back to his office to talk with me and fill out his report to the dean. But when I got back to the library and turned around to see where he wanted us to go, I was very surprised to find he wasn't there. I assumed he had a few things to take care of before he joined me. But the minutes ticked by and Mr. Murray didn't appear. I let five minutes pass and decided that, for some reason, he had chosen not to catch up with me.

I reported to class that day at the usual time. Mr. Murray was writing our homework assignment on the blackboard and didn't seem to notice me. He apparently never reported the incident, never even brought it up to me. I wonder if Mr. Murray and I were birds of a feather. He said my skipping convocation was ridiculous, and the feeling was mutual. You never know where you'll meet a fellow ghost—perhaps in a small room at the end of an empty hall.

CHAPTER 5

The Operation

Post Parting

You ask how I'm doing:
imagine it's midnight,
and I'm strolling the deck
of an ocean liner
far out at sea.
A luminous moon smiles down
from a velvet sky,
the soft mantle of a world at peace.
Suddenly the ship lurches,
and I fly over the railing,
plummeting through the cool night air,
silent as a feather,
past lighted portholes
and the sounds of distant laughter.
I drop into the black water
with an almost inaudible splash,
colored lanterns swinging

from wrought-iron trellises,
the cheerful sounds of an orchestra
drifting over the swells.
The ship sails on,
plowing gently through the waves.
Say the ship was my world.
Does that answer your question?

One December morning that year, I reported to the nurse's office for my annual physical. I was sitting on the bench next to the nurse's desk, waiting to see the doctor, a man I didn't know from Adam, or anyone else, and whom I was not likely to see again. One of my classmates, a boy named Carlton came out of the examination room and walked past me without a word. He looked a little bothered, which worried me. But I figured he just wasn't happy about being prodded in private places by someone other than his girlfriend. I didn't even know if he had one. Jennifer Bates was the closest I had come, and that wasn't very close.

"Your turn," the school nurse said to me brightly. I got up from the bench and walked to the examination room. The doctor, a middle-aged man with a silver beard, was sitting at the desk. He didn't look up as he waved me in.

"Please sit on the table," the doctor said to me as he leafed through a stack of forms, his voice heavy with boredom. In a minute, he walked over and began a quick physical exam, which included lightly pressing his stethoscope to my chest and listening for a few seconds, feeling the glands in my neck, shining a light in my ears and looking inside for moment. Then he had me stand and put his finger against my crotch. He told me to cough. He took a step back and looked at me. "Have you ever had a hernia?" he asked. I shook my head. "Well, you have one now."

A few weeks later, my parents drove me to the hospital several towns away. It was early in the morning and a light snow was falling. That week, I would discover that being sick won me attention, something I almost (like most people, I suppose) rarely refused. In the hospital, I would dimly see that illness opened some doors for me. That's probably when I first started wondering, unconsciously, what role my body might be playing in my getting sick or *pretending* I am.

After checking in at the hospital's front desk, I was transferred to a wheelchair by a friendly, young, male attendant. He took me to the elevator, with my parents walking behind us. We went up one flight, then the doors opened, and he took me to my room.

"I feel like I'm going to a funeral," I said to him, joking. "Mine."

"You'll do great," he said brightly. "What are you here for? I know we're not supposed to ask people that, but I can't help wondering."

"They're going to correct my hernia," I answered.

"That'll be a snap," he assured me. "I bet they do that all the time."

"Yeah, probably," I said. "I just wish they were doing one less this year."

My parents had followed me into my room. I turned to them, "What's with the empty bed?" I asked my father, pointing at them. "Am I going to have a roommate?"

"Probably," said my father.

"What if I get some real weirdo?" I said. All I knew for sure was that I wanted out of the hospital, preferably before the operation. Dread had started dripping into my veins. I usually love to travel, but I wasn't looking forward to a trip to the operating room. A nurse helped me to bed, and began doing all kinds of things nurses do. After a few hours, my parents watched as an orderly rolled me away into the operating room, promising they'd be there when I rolled back in.

After I came back from the recovery ward, I was back in my room, which was thankfully still unoccupied. I was joined by one nurse, then another and the two helped me into the bed. My mother and father entered the room and stood there looking at me.

"How are you doing?" my father asked me.

"I have this bad pain in my stomach."

My father turned to one of the nurses. "He's in a little pain," he said. "Can you give him something for it?"

"I'll talk with the doctor," the nurse said and left the room.

A few minutes later, she came back in and from a pocket of her gown, she withdrew a syringe. "I'm going to give you something for the pain," she said. "You'll feel a little sting when the needle goes in, but it won't hurt. Then you're going to feel a whole lot better, I promise." She had me turn onto my side and gave me a shot of euphoria. Morphine. In a minute, I felt better than I ever knew I could.

I left the hospital a few days later and went home. My father walked with me to the second floor and into my bedroom. He helped me put on my pajamas and accompanied me to the den. After we entered the room, my parents draped a blanket over me and helped me lie down on the sofa. Then they left the room and headed downstairs. My mother returned by herself, holding a glass bowl filled with chocolate stars, my favorite candy. She placed the bowl on the table next to me and smoothed down the blanket. On the table, she lay down a book about John Wilkes Booth and the assassination of Lincoln, a piece of American history that had long fascinated me.

My mother sat down in her easy chair next to the window and continued working on her jigsaw puzzle of wooden sailboats on a blue lake. For once, there was no noise in the house from a TV, radio, or record player. I stared out the window, enjoying the peace. I took in the brilliant patches of snow on the garage roof and the newly white trunks of the trees in the yard. All was silent and still, and I felt happy.

In some dark corner of my mind, I might have believed I'd stumbled on the secret of gaining my parents' love. Eventually, I would come to know they had always felt the deepest concern for my well-being and happiness. My parents simply weren't very good at showing it. I decided I could lend them, and myself, a hand and seal my happy fate. My being in the hospital brought the depth of their feelings for me into unfamiliar focus. It's not hard to see why I might have considered being sick as a magical elixir for opening the heart. Being healthy hadn't seemed to work. Maybe being sick was the answer.

CHAPTER 6

Jumping To Conclusions

Portrait in Pastel

She travels to places I'll never see
save on her canvas,
making the fibers breathe
in tones richer than memory.
She abandons herself in hues—
the burnt orange, soft magenta, and steaming rose of a
   sunset.
Color defines her desires,
making them sparkle like shooting stars.
She traces delicate patterns
that infuse life into the contours of her rapture
and floats melody into the mist.
Sometimes she's laughing in my dreams,
helping to protect the innocence
of a child's blueprint of the world.
Days she isn't here,
every room is too big

and crowded with emptiness.
She ignites the air with her brush
cradling the flawless complexion of the world.

After school one April afternoon, I left my first-grade class and met Claudia and Christian, on the front walk of our grammar school. As we meandered down the hill, we saw our mother driving up Kings Road in her 4-door Oldsmobile. When we reached the bottom of the walk, the school crossing guard—stout, friendly Auntie Mary—waved our little group forward. We crossed the street and stepped onto the curb on the other side; our mother's car glided to a stop several yards away, on the shoulder of the street; it was rare that our mother picked us up at school on a sunny, spring day. We usually walked the half-mile home. So I wondered why today was different.

Once we had piled into the back seat and shut the door, our mother turned around and looked at us.

"We're going to have another mouth to feed in our family soon," she quietly announced.

"When?" my brother asked with a grin.

"In a few months," my mother answered.

"Yay!" my sister cried happily.

My mother smiled and took us home. This development would shortly turn my whole life around. The news delighted my brother and sister, but I wasn't happy at all. I felt Chris and I were plenty of boys for our family, and I certainly didn't want another sister. I knew the additional sibling was bound to be a rival for my parents' attention and affection and sensed I would soon be ousted from my position as baby of the family. After six years of being virtually untouchable, I was about to be replaced, relegated to an unthinkable invisibility in my parents' eyes.

Though I didn't know it, I would soon begin a ruthless, but slyly undetectable campaign to destroy my younger sibling in every way legally possible. I would need to prevent my parents from finding out that I was harboring, and intending to implement, enormous ill-will toward the new arrival. It was crucial that I appear completely innocent in my parents' eyes. And I would have to convince them that my nemesis was not my equal in any way.

It would take me years to fully accept my demotion in the family order. I know that such brother-sister rivalries are common and natural, but I still feel a little embarrassed by the resilience of my struggle. One day, when Tracy (my little, highly unwelcome sister) was six, I had taken my post outside her bedroom door, a devilish grin on my face. I had just arrived at the beautiful idea of plotting an evil scheme out loud, pretending I didn't know she was there.

"I'll ask her to come to the bathroom to see something amazing," I said, loudly and clearly. "I'll be standing there when she comes into the room, and I'll ask her to lean out the window and look down, that I wanted her to see something incredible." I was sure she was listening to me breathlessly, with something close to terror. "When her shoulders are over the windowsill," I continued, "I'll come up behind and push her out."

I let a few seconds pass, then called to her, "Hey Trace," I said, "come here a second. I want to show something amazing!" She ran screaming down the stairs, no doubt convinced I was going to kill her. 'Mission accomplished,' I must have been feeling on some level.

On another occasion, my whole family was sitting in the

den watching TV. Tracy was up front close to the screen and I sat on the end of the couch, a few feet away. When it seemed no one was paying any attention, I scraped something out of my nose with a fingernail and flicked it to the side. A moment later, Tracy held up her hand and looked at the back of it, scrunching her nose in disbelief. What had just been on *my* finger was now, miraculously, on *hers*.

"How did *that* get there?!" she almost shrieked, holding up her hand. My father looked over and saw the situation.

"Tracy, that's disgusting!" he bellowed. "Go to the bathroom and wash your hands this instant!"

She immediately got up from the carpet and turned to the door. As she rushed past me, she managed to shoot me an accusatory glance. She knew I was involved somehow, but we both knew she would never be able be able to prove it. It was another major victory in my crusade to drive her from a status of near perfection.

Life sometimes hands people a dose of what they've dished out to others. During Christmas break from my freshman year of my little state college in Pennsylvania, I lived with Tracy and our mother at our childhood home on Kings Road. Tracy was just a block away for a few days, house-sitting for a friend's mother. My parents had separated a year before, my father having moved to an apartment across town. Claudia and Christian were beginning their adult lives in other parts of the country, Claudia in college and Chris working at a country club with a friend in Palm Beach, Florida.

My mother had been getting anonymous phone calls for a couple of weeks. The man who called wasn't big on small talk: he always came right to the point. According to him, my father was sleeping with another woman (who happened to be his wife). He told my mother that if she wanted to catch her husband, she just had to go to a certain motel on the highway and wait. Sleep hadn't come easily to my mother since marrying my father who snored like a buzz saw. (I had been a nervous child, and his snoring reassured me that all was right with the world.) The telephone calls rattled my mother and made it hard for her to sleep, even though my noisy father no longer shared her bed.

My mother came into my room at 2:00 that morning, put her hand on my shoulder, and not so gently shoved me. I awoke abruptly and peered up into her face, which was only a few inches from mine.

"He's *here*!" she whispered sharply.

"Who's here?" I said, groggily, wiping the sleep out of my eyes.

"The *madman*!" she hissed. "*You* know!"

I didn't know and stared at her blankly. "Oh come on!" she exclaimed in a fierce whisper. "The anonymous phone calls?! The man who tells me that I should go to the motel and catch your father in the act?!" That highly disturbing image had already burrowed deeply into my brain.

The doorbell suddenly started to ring and kept ringing for several seconds. I looked at my mother in some alarm. "It's *him*!" she crowed. "I *know* it is!"

"OK, OK!" I whispered. "I'll call the police." I put one foot in the hall and waited to see if the doorbell would ring again. I looked down through the banister at the front door. The house was silent; all I heard was the ticking of my clock. Suddenly the doorbell rang again. The sound shook me and I took a step backward into the bedroom.

"What are you *doing?*" my mother hissed again, punching

me on the arm. "I thought you were calling the police!"

"I am! I am!" I whispered hotly, as the doorbell continued to ring. I left my room and walked swiftly down the corridor to the den. The doorbell rang a few more times as I opened the phone book and found the number of the police station. I immediately dialed it.

"Police station."

"There's a man on the front porch, and he's ringing the doorbell!" I said a little breathlessly.

"Can you see the man?"

"No," I told him

"How do you know it's a man?"

"Some guy has been making harassing phone calls to my mother," I returned with annoyance. "It has to be him down there! Can you guys *please* come over right away? My mother's a nervous wreck!"

In a moment the officer assured me that a car would be over in a few minutes. I hung up the phone and hustled back down the corridor. My mother was standing in the shadows of my bedroom, looking terrified. I stopped at the edge of the hall and peeked down at the thin glass strips on either side of the front door but couldn't see anything. Now the doorbell rang again. I looked over at my mother. She was staring at me in terror. "They're coming!" I shot back, hoping it would calm her.

The doorbell had been ringing continuously for over a minute when I saw red lights pulsing in the driveway and breathed a sigh of relief. In a moment, I heard the sound of boots crunching gravel. I came out from behind the wall and headed for the stairs. My mother looked enormously relieved and gave me a thin smile as I passed. When I approached the front door, I could hear the policeman talking on the porch. I couldn't hear the other man; I wondered if he had gone silent now that the jig was up and he would soon be on his way to jail.

I unbolted the door and slowly swung it back. There stood the policeman, still talking to the shadowy figure, who had his back to the door. He was much shorter than I expected, and his sweater looked familiar. In a moment I realized why. When the person turned around, I saw it wasn't a man at all and far from a stranger. It was Tracy, and her eyes were daggers. I looked from her to the policeman, who seemed to be enjoying the whole thing.

"Are you all set then?" he asked me with a wry smile.

"Yes," I replied sheepishly. "Thank you, Officer."

My sister didn't say a word to me when she entered the house. She immediately went into the bathroom and banged the door closed behind her.

I waited a few moments then called to her. "Can I get you anything, Trace?"

"Shut up" she said.

CHAPTER 7

Down The Stairs

Who Poured The Light?

Who poured the light into your eyes,
the hallowed, unyielding light
and taught you to hold up your hands
against fragments raining down from the fractured sky?
You walked the ocean floor
choked by remorse over outcomes
you could not have prevented.
But the puddles beneath your feet have dried,
and your sky no longer drips ash.
You've begun walking a fresh path,
drinking in the promise
that everything is possible

and all your graves have begun to bloom.

At 27, I was living on the third floor of my mother's duplex, one town away from where I grew up. There were three of us living in her house—my mother, Tracy, and I. My parents had been divorced for over a year, and my father lived by himself in the next town. He was glad to be free and on his own, but my mother was still recovering from his decision to leave. She was always looking for a reason to call him. That April night, I gave her one.

    Tracy had a room on the second floor, at the other end of the short hallway leading to my mother's room. The two of them were sound asleep when I came back from a friend's house just after eleven. I had been feeling a little apprehensive all day, as though something had entered the cells of my body and was starting to make its way out. I walked quietly through my mother's bedroom and climbed the stairs to my room on the third floor. I thought I'd probably feel better after a good night's sleep and quickly undressed. I threw on a T-shirt and a pair of sweat pants and got into my bed. I opened the window. to get fresh air into my lungs, then gazed up at the stars; they shone dimly through a wispy layer of clouds.

    As I lay down, a car passed slowly through the neighborhood. I pulled the pillow under my head, and quickly fell asleep. A few hours later I woke with a start. I knew something was about to happen to me, something bad. I didn't know what it was; I just knew I didn't want to be alone.

    I spun out of bed and hurried across the floor. A moment later, I blacked out and began to fall forward. I didn't feel myself tumble down the stairs. When I clumped onto the floor of my mother's bedroom, she quickly awoke in terror and reached for her bedside lamp. Her hands were shaking so badly she couldn't immediately put her fingers on the light switch. I woke up on a stretcher with an EMT standing over me.

    When my mind cleared, I realized that Tracy was kneeling beside me; she looked concerned but was smiling and stroking my forehead.

"Am I dying?" I asked her.

"No, you're not dying," she said softly with a comforting smile. "You had a nasty fall. We'll find out why when we get to the hospital."

"We're going to the hospital?" I asked, still a little confused about what was happening. "How come?"

"That's usually where people go when they've fallen and don't know why." She continued stroking my forehead.

The EMTs carried me out of my mother's room on a stretcher; we passed Tracy's room on our way to the stairs. I glanced in and saw my mother with her back pressed against the wall, her hand over her mouth. My father stood at her side; he wasn't holding her hand, wasn't touching her in any way. As I was being carried past, I felt an uncomfortable emptiness where sadness would have been if I'd allowed myself to feel it.

The EMTs carried me onto the landing and down the steps. When they bore me through the living room and onto the front porch, I turned my head and saw the ambulance idling in the driveway, its red lights slowly revolving. The two men opened the rear door of the vehicle and gently slid me into the back. The driver turned the key and started the engine, and we began to move. From the corner of my eye, I saw my father's car following us which put me somewhat at ease. The other man had taken a seat beside me and asked how I was feeling. I told him I was doing fine, and he said he was going to start an IV.

"What's that for?" I asked him.

"We're just going to get some fluids into you."

At the hospital, I was quickly taken to a room in the emergency ward and lifted onto the bed. I lay there watching nurses, interns, and others walk past. Eventually a nurse came by, asked me how I was feeling, what had happened, and if I thought I'd broken anything. She asked me my name, the year, and if I knew where I was.

"What happened to me?" I asked her.

"We're going to try and find out," she answered. "We'll do a few tests and have you talk to a doctor." At that moment, my worried parents and sister found me.

"What happened to him?" my father asked the nurse anxiously.

"We're going to find out, Sir."

In a little while, I was sent downstairs for a CAT scan to get pictures of the inside of my skull. Then they returned me to my room and told us a doctor would be in soon. My mother sat wringing her hands for an hour, until the neurologist walked in. He was a soft-spoken, middle-aged man and was wearing a white hospital gown. He greeted us in a friendly voice.

"What happened to me?" I asked him immediately.

"You had a grand mal seizure," he answered. "But keep in mind, people have seizures for lots of reasons, not all of them that serious. We've given you blood tests, an EKG, a CAT scan, and there doesn't seem to be anything to worry about. I think you're going to be fine."

The blood came back into my mother's face. Tracy took her hand. My father stood next to the bed and laid a hand on my arm.

What happened that night was the calling card of MS, a neurological disease that steadily gnaws away at the myelin sheath, a fatty substance that covers and protects the nerves. No one suspected my seizure was a sign that the disease had begun its work: it would keep a low profile in me for many years.

In the hospital, I stayed in a room for the night so the staff could make sure I wasn't in any danger. A doctor prescribed an anti-convulsant drug to prevent me from having more seizures.

The following morning, they sent me home. My father picked me up and walked me to the parking lot.

"Feeling better?" he asked.

"Yeah, I feel fine," I replied. "The doctor didn't think there was anything seriously wrong."

"Yes, he said that in the vast majority of cases a person never gets another one."

"Yeah, something like that. I sure hope he's right," I replied.

"I'm sure you don't have anything to worry about."

My father always tried to put a positive spin on things, as it made him lighter and happier and less likely to tumble into emotional sinkholes. He was determined to live above dark terrain as much as he could.

My Father

What do you see up there, father
three stories above me
on the roof of my world?
The sun in your face
lights up things unspoken—
frustration, regret,
the life that got away
despite your noblest intentions.

In your butter-yellow shirt,
stained with the leafy mold of rotting gutters;
you stand within reach of heaven,
high above a world of mute, suburban longing
and stillborn dreams.
Dear father,
I swear to you,
until this moment
I never thought
God could know anything but
serene contentment
among the happy birds
and green clouds
of the maple trees.

My mother, on the other hand, didn't seem able to forgive the world for allowing certain things to happen. When I was about ten, her nephew Michael lived with us for a year. Claudia has the best memory in the family and remembers everything, including things she wants to forget. She said Michael made us laugh a lot. He introduced her to the Beatles, and she talked with him about bands he liked and the great concerts he'd seen. Claudia told me Michael was very likable. He and my mother became close that year. Soon after graduating from Dayton College and moving to an apartment with his girlfriend, Michael started having Grand Mal seizures. They found a malignant tumor in his brain; Michael died a couple of years later.

Tragedy started early in my mother's life. When she was a young teenager, her brother returned from the Korean War and got involved with a married woman. It didn't end well. After a few weeks, she broke it off with him and thought that would be the end of things. One night, after bowling with her friends, she walked to the parking lot to get into her car. As she was going through her purse for the keys, my uncle emerged from behind a parked car, shot and killed her, then turned the gun on himself.

A few years after this, my mother's world was rocked by another tragedy. On a cold winter night, her father was walking home from the bar, very drunk, as he often was. When he got home, he began to climb the porch steps and suddenly collapsed and banged his head. He lay unconscious on the porch for a long time in the frigid night. By the time he came to, he had begun running a fever. A few days later he died of pneumonia. My mother blamed herself for these losses. She seemed to blame herself for a lot of things that weren't anyone's fault.

One snowy December evening after my seizure, during the winter Tracy and I lived with our mother in Chatham, my mother and I were walking down the block together. We both loved watching the snow float and drop a blanket on the ground. She was in a quiet, reflective mood; I had a feeling some questions were coming. We got to the top of the street and stopped for a moment to take in the scene.

"Do you remember Michael?" she asked me, speaking of her nephew.

"Not really," I said. "I was just a kid when he lived with us. What was I? Nine, ten?"

"About ten."

"Why did he move in with us, anyway? You probably told me, but I forgot."

"He was Ruth and Johnny's son. And he wanted out of there. Ruth and Johnny were terrible drunks."

Ruth was my mother's half-sister. She was adamantly opposed to my mother marrying Roger, my father. Ruth told my mother that this Roger guy was no good and not to be trusted. After my father left the marriage, my mother never spoke to Ruth again.

"I think tragedy follows me," my mother said. "I wonder what I did to deserve it. I broke a man's heart when I was young. Maybe that was it. He wanted to marry me, and I almost did. I probably should have."

"How come you didn't?" I asked her.

"I met your father." Neither of us spoke for a little while. "I was definitely a fool. But then I wouldn't have had you guys. I can't imagine that."

I'm sure she couldn't have imagined flicking on her lamp in the middle of the night to find me on her floor in a full-blown seizure. She probably never saw Michael in the grip of one, but I don't doubt she thought of him that night. Nor do I doubt she once more blamed herself.

Suddenly I remembered that my mother used to fall into fits of uncontrollable laughter without warning. It could happen anywhere and for no obvious reason. We would laugh along with her, but I always wanted her hysterics to end sooner than they usually did. I felt a little sorry for my mother, with all her secrets and hidden emotions. Who was she? Where was she? I wanted to reach her, but I couldn't. Given the tragedies that swept through her family, she wanted to remain in control of her feelings. She believed that taking her hands off the wheel would allow the swells of grief to pull her under.

One night, several months after my diagnosis, she called me. For a few moments there was an awkward silence between us.

"Is everything OK, Mom? It's really late for you."

"I caused your MS," she said softly, but with an air of conviction.

"Don't be ridiculous, Mom!" I said, almost scolding her. "This is nobody's fault. Certainly not yours." I hoped my mother would come to believe me.

I suddenly remembered the beautiful spring day I had walked home from the grammar school alone. When I entered the dining room, I heard a woman singing beautifully from the radio in the hallway above me. I climbed the stairs to hear the magical singing more clearly. I wanted to find out who it was. When I reached the landing, I looked through the banister. I realized at once, the radio wasn't even on; my mother was standing at the ironing board, singing. I couldn't believe she was capable of making such a heavenly sound. In church on Sunday, I'd never really heard her sing. She'd always stood beside my father who sang loudly, and not terribly well. He and the voices on all sides of us drowned her out. I looked at my mother that day and quietly gasped. She heard me and turned. Seeing me there, she instantly stopped without a word. I never heard her sing again.

That day, I realized I was missing someone I'd never even met. My mother had a beauty I didn't know existed, something she kept to herself. She never allowed that beauty to shine in front of anyone; I was lucky enough to stumble upon it, but the tragedies of her life caused her such shame, how could she allow beauty in, except in secret?

In time I would come to miss someone I used to know quite well. In several years I'd come to feel like asking my body why it had so forcefully turned against me. Of course, my body was not capable of responding, but it wouldn't have mattered anyway; my disease seems to go about its business without feeling a need to explain itself. Afraid that asking too many questions would bring me bad news, I avoided asking any. In time, I would even ignore signs that probably should have gotten my attention.

CHAPTER 8

Shakespeare in New Jersey

Ivory

I have watched you sitting against ivory
followed your fingers as they dance over the keys.
You carry songs in your head;
sometimes I wonder what else you have in there.
Lucky, the ones who know
or will.
With hands on the rudder
you are marking your course
over the ocean swells
and have already begun
gliding through the sunshine
past fields of flowers
and green, waving grass.
You won't see it
but I'll be waving, too.

In the June I turned 27, a few months before I was due to leave for graduate school, I started looking for a way to make some extra money. One morning I was scanning the help wanted section of the paper and found an ad from an elderly woman who needed someone to drive her to the post office, library, grocery store, and various appointments. Her name was Ethel Saltus, and she lived by herself minutes away from me.

    I called the number in the paper and talked to a guy named Kevin who had been driving Miss Saltus around for a couple weeks and seemed eager to find a replacement. Very eager. He gave me directions to her house and said he would call and tell her I'd be coming the next day to meet her. The following afternoon, I drove a few miles to a small village on the edge of the woods. I turned into a driveway just past the center of town; it curved through tall bushes with branches that scraped the sides of the car as I passed. Ahead of me stood an aging, yellow, Victorian house. A riot of leaves and vines pressed against its walls and windows, as though wanting to get inside.

    I parked next to the side porch, got out of the car, and looked around. The yard was a jungle of vegetation, and miscellaneous items were strewn about; the arm of a wooden chair, a rusted watering can, the top of a broken trellis, a rusted window screen. A hundred feet away stood the shell of an old barn. Swallows raced in and out of gaping holes in walls that were no longer perpendicular to the ground. From inside the house came a mechanical hum and metallic clicking. In a few minutes, the sound stopped, and through the screen I heard a shuffling sound like sandpaper on wood. Then a face appeared at the screen door. Her hair was a shade of orange I'd never seen on a human head.

    "Who's that?" she cried in a shrill falsetto that suggested British aristocracy. With her white face looking out from a dark and crumbling old house, she reminded me of Miss Havisham from *Great Expectations*. Ethel Saltus lived by herself in a shadowy world of dark shapes and endless clutter.

"Hi. My name is Keith, (I hadn't yet started going by Sean, my actual first name) and I'm interested in becoming your new driver."

"How lovely!" She was apparently pleased that she might have a new face in her world.

Miss Saltus (as she instructed me to call her) emerged and stood on the porch. She eyed me and smiled. "How do you *do?*" she sang out. "Hand!" she barked at me suddenly, looking down at the porch steps in front of her. I immediately stepped over and climbed a couple of stairs. Then I offered her my arm, which Miss Saltus clamped onto at the wrist. Gripping the banister with her other hand, she started cautiously down the stairs. When she reached the ground, I stepped back and took my first good look at Ethel Saltus. She stood around 5'7" and had large and striking blue eyes, the lashes thick with mascara. The line she had drawn under her eyes with eyeliner was too low and a little crooked. Her mouth was small and round, and her lips were painted bright red, which contrasted sharply with the pallor of her face.

"My you're tall!" she smiled, then she shuffled past me to the passenger door and stopped, waiting for me to open it. I quickly took my cue and swung the door open wide. "Why thank you," she cooed. "What a gentleman!"

We had barely reached the end of the driveway when my nose was hit by a powerful stench. "What is that *smell?*" I cried, thinking we might have just rolled over a dead animal.

"What?!" Miss Saltus exclaimed, stretching out the word while the pitch climbed ever higher, as though she'd just heard news of an unimaginable scandal.

"Oh, it's nothing," I said, having instantly realized the odor was emanating from Miss Saltus herself. "Whatever it was, we're past it," I said. Abruptly, I wasn't sure I could do the job, even if it was a very easy way to make some money. I was pretty sure Miss Saltus had an inkling as to the true source of the smell and was happy to have herself ruled out. I opened my window, which dissipated the odor in a few minutes, and we continued on our way to the post office, the first stop she wanted to make.

Upon pulling into the parking lot, she handed me the key to her mailbox; I went in quickly and opened it. The mailbox was empty, save for a few pieces of junk mail. (This would be the case almost every day for the three months I worked for her.) Returning to the car, I asked Miss Saltus where she wanted to go next.

She raised a hand. "I'm tired," she said. "Take me home, please."

When I dropped her off, I got out of the car, walked around it, and opened the door for her. She stood up and turned toward me. "Same time tomorrow?" she asked.

"Absolutely," I said, nodding with false enthusiasm, as if I was glad we'd soon be driving together again. She opened the kitchen door and stepped inside. My introduction to Miss Saltus had ended.

The next morning, Kevin dropped off Miss Saltus' yellow Ford. In a little while, I was off to my first full day of work with her. I was glad for the use of her car, (she wouldn't stink up mine) and it made me feel better about taking the job, although I still didn't know if I should.

That morning I pulled into her driveway a few minutes before nine. I knocked on the kitchen door and waited for her to appear. Soon, she opened the door, walked onto the porch, and smiled at me.

"Here we are again!" she chirped. "I'm so glad you decided to return. Did you think maybe you wouldn't?"

"Of course not!" I lied. I helped her down the stairs and into the car's passenger seat. Then I went around, opened my door and got in the car myself.

"You're a good man," she said. "A good *young* man. And that's saying a lot."

"I take it you don't think much of young men," I said with a smile.

"Well, don't you think a good percentage of them leave a bit to be desired. In the sense of character, I mean. I don't think you're one of those."

"Thank you." I said. "But you really don't know me. I could be a mass murderer."

"Don't be foolish," she said. "I get a reliable sense of people the moment I meet them. I liked you right away."

Miss Saltus was wearing a change of clothes, which probably accounted for my not being assaulted by that horrendous aroma. The rest of the morning passed. I had begun to feel better about working for her.

I went back to Miss Saltus' house the following morning. I pulled into her driveway and got out of the car. I rang the doorbell and waited a few minutes. She failed to appear, so I let myself into the kitchen and called her name. Again, she didn't respond. I looked around. The kitchen was shrouded in semi-darkness, but after a minute, my eyes had adjusted. The table was littered with dishes, one of which held half-eaten chicken pieces. I saw an open package of ground beef, a saucepan full of soup, a pint carton of cream standing in a white puddle, a grimy glass beside an uncapped, half-empty bottle of King William Scotch. One of the chairs was pulled out from the table and on the seat was a bowl of melted ice cream. A chicken bone lay on the floor beneath a chair. The sink was piled high with dishes on which the remains of meals were hardening. On the counter sat more dishes and another open bottle of whiskey. A small pile of food cartons and tin cans had collected next to the overflowing garbage pail in the corner. Within moments, I had developed a powerful aversion to touching anything in the room. I decided not to wake her should she be sleeping; I hoped she was. After quickly leaving the house, I got in the car and drove home.

The next morning, Miss Saltus was absent from the porch again. I climbed the stairs and looked through the kitchen window. She was nowhere to be seen. I walked to the front hall and stopped at the bottom of the stairs again.

This time she called down to me before I spoke: "Keith, is that you?"

"Yes, it's me," I answered, a little relieved.

"Wait a minute," she said. "I'll be right down. Go outside and wait for me on the porch."

Her speech was heavily garbled and came from the back of her throat. I went outside, stood on the bottom step and waited. Rather than go back into the kitchen, I stepped onto the side porch and sat down on a white wicker bench, which buckled under my weight. I kept one ear cocked for the sound of her chair lift descending; I saw that the floorboards beneath me sagged badly; the whole area looked as though it might cave in at any moment. After five minutes, I went back inside and called Miss Saltus once again. This time there was no reply. I thought about the two half empty bottles of King William sitting on the kitchen table and thought Miss Saltus was probably asleep and that it was pointless to call to her again. I walked back through the kitchen, got into my car and drove home.

When I returned at two o'clock, Miss Saltus was sitting at the kitchen table in front of a now nearly empty bottle of liquor. She didn't look like the same person I'd seen the day before.

"You were supposed to be here an hour ago," she snarled at me as I came in the door. I told her I had been there and that I had called to her but never got a reply. "Oh, don't give me that!" she almost shouted. Pressing down on the arms of her chair, she got unsteadily to her feet. She peered around the room and asked me if I could find her bag. It sat on the table before her, two feet from her hand.

"Here it is, Miss Saltus," I said. She was rocking on her heels, holding onto the back of her chair with one hand, making chewing sounds with her mouth. Her tan raincoat hung over a chair in the corner. She told me to help her put it on, stepped away from it to the chair, and gripped the edge of the counter. When I brought her the coat, my nose was hit once more by the reek of urine. I held out her coat without breathing, and when she pushed her arms through the sleeves, I picked up her bag and escaped to the porch. Suddenly, I understood why Kevin had told me next to nothing about Miss Saltus' personal hygiene, which was virtually non-existent. In the entire three months I worked for her, I never saw a sign that she had stepped into a bathtub. She wore the same clothes for days in a row, turning her pants and shirt inside out when she couldn't remove the stains. There were often remnants of a meal hanging from her blouse, and the stench of her urine would drive customers out the door of small shops. She regularly did and said shocking things in public. One day I watched her pull the legs off a rotisserie chicken, take a few bites, and place it on a shelf as she passed. Afterwards, we were sitting in her car in the store's parking lot, and a woman walked past. "What an interesting dress," Miss Saltus said to her. "Oh, do you like it?" the woman asked. "I hate it!" Miss Saltus snarled.

I soon came to the conclusion that King William ruled her life. Whenever she was drunk, which was a good deal of the time, she turned nasty, even cruel. One day she asked me who my favorite writers were and then mocked my choices. Another day, I made the mistake of telling her I played the piano and wrote songs. "And I suppose you think you're an artist!" she sneered. "It's all nonsense!"

Two weeks after I started working for Miss Saltus, I felt I'd had enough and decided to take an ad out in the same paper Kevin had used to get his freedom back. It was a rainy Monday morning when I pulled up her driveway. Miss Saltus walked onto the porch and began tying the strings of her rain hat. I was sullen and stayed in the car choosing not to help her down the stairs. She must have immediately gauged my mood, as she started down the rain-slicked stairs by herself, gripping the banister tightly. When she touched down on the second step, her foot slid out from under her, and she fell heavily on her side. Rolling over once, arms flailing, she bumped down onto the next step and bounced off the porch, ending up sitting in a large ceramic pot on the bottom stair. Leaping out of the car I raced to her side, thinking I had probably killed her.

"Are you hurt?" I cried, kneeling in the mud and seized her by the shoulders. She was pushing down on the rim of the pot, trying to free herself. I grabbed her under the arms and heaved her off the ground, but the pot came with her.

She calmly ordered me to get behind her. I moved over, grabbed her under her arms, placed my foot on the rim of the pot and heaved once more. This time I succeeded in pulling her off the pot and onto her feet. With a firm grip on her arm, I led her to the car and sat her down on the front seat. When she raised her head to look at me, I saw blood inching down her cheek from the corner of her eye. Above her lower lid a red pool was forming. I felt my knees go weak. I told her there was blood coming out of one of her eyes, fully expecting my words would make her faint. Without emotion, she asked how much blood there was, as it dripped onto her blouse. She touched her cheek and looked at her finger, then told me to get her a wet paper towel. I dashed into the kitchen, tore one off the roll and brought it out to her. She gently dabbed the skin around her eye and looked at the towel every so often to see if the bleeding had stopped. She didn't seem the least bit alarmed.

"How does my eye look?" she asked me

"It looks good" I answered, relieved.

She studied my face. After a moment, she said, "You look pale."

"I was afraid you were hurt," I said.

My words seemed to amaze her. Miss Saltus looked astonished that someone actually cared whether she lived or died. "That would actually have mattered to you?" she asked.

Of course," I told her.

At her insistence, we took a peaceful drive through the countryside. She said it might get some color back in my cheeks. The sky had stopped dripping, and the sun stretched golden bars to the earth, lighting up some of the trees and patches of hillside. Miss Saltus told me how she loved the light green tips of the pine needles, and that she'd never seen anything more beautiful than the yellow roadside lilies.

And that's when my feelings about her changed. Until ten o'clock that morning, I saw her only as a pitiful old alcoholic who needed more help than I was qualified or willing to give. I wanted to get far away from her and never think about her again. But after her fall, I hardly recognized her; she was taking care of *me*.

It had taken me a while to see that she had a quirky playfulness. One morning, something caught my eye: beside the cellar door, the lifeless head and shoulders of a large, brown rat were sticking out of a crack in the base of the wall. Its eyes and mouth were frozen open, and terror was written on its face, as though death had seized the animal from behind. Still horrified by it days later, I told Miss Saltus what I had seen. Without missing a beat, she turned to me with an impish grin and said, "Not surprising, dear—my house is on a rat migration route."

With Miss Saltus there was always more than met the eye. I remember sitting on a park bench with her, studying the sky. "Do you ever watch the clouds in their endless parade?" she asked. I told her that I loved to look at them and then asked her which word was better, endless or never-ending. "Dear boy," she said, "does it really matter?" In her way, she was often asking me that question.

Miss Saltus adored flowers and could identify them on sight. Looking out the car window as we were driving through the countryside one day, she spotted a bed of peonies.

"The peony wanted to be a rose but never quite made it. Don't be a peony, my dear," she said to me.

A few minutes later she mentioned the fiancé she had when she was a young woman. "I loved him so much," she said with a sigh. "But I don't think love was enough for him. Not mine, at least."

One day she went into the living room closet and pulled out a trunk of her theatre costumes. "I was an actress, you know," she said proudly. "Does that surprise you?"

"Almost nothing about you surprises me anymore," I told her.

Once she asked me what my favorite flower was. "The lilac," I answered.

"That's one of my favorites, too," she said. She was silent for a while, then she said something that pleased me, though I knew I would never tell her. "You're a lilac to me," she said. "My lilac."

One day, we returned to her house after a drive and rolled to a stop at the end of her driveway. I was in no hurry to leave, so I turned off the engine, and we sat together in the car. Miss Saltus was looking off at the broken-down barn, watching the swallows flitting in and out under the roof. Then she quoted *Hamlet*. "There is special providence in the fall of a sparrow," she began. She was silent for a few moments then continued. "If it be now, 'tis not to come; if it be not now, yet it will come—the readiness is all."

I later found out that Miss Saltus had been educated at Radcliffe and at the Sorbonne in Paris. I hadn't known the caliber of the person I had been driving and cleaning up after. Miss Saltus had been living in a squalor that seeped into her mind and marred her dignity. It seemed that after the fall, she drank less, though my memory might have been no more reliable than hers. Voltaire may have gotten it right when he called history, "tricks we play on the dead." One thing I know for sure is that after her fall we talked more often and took many long rides in the countryside around Green Village.

"I'm a great believer," Miss Saltus once told me—squinting down the road, as if the words were coming into sight—"in the idea that some cases of serious illness are caused by a blow to the spirit." At the time, I didn't give it much thought. But now I think she may have been right.

On our last day together, I helped Miss Saltus out of the car and up the stairs to the porch stairs I'd let her descend by herself one rainy morning. We stood together for a minute, then she took my hand and squeezed it. "Didn't we have fun, Rotkehlchen?" It was German for robin redbreast and a name she called me in honor of the rust-colored jacket I wore.

"Yes, we did," I answered.

"And you'll come and see me?"

"Of course." I felt the end of my nose start to tingle. Miss Saltus gave me a long look, patted my hand, and disappeared inside.

CHAPTER 9

Third Floor

Dust

The dust is knee-deep in these rooms
  I have come to see
  if there are any shadows
  I might recognize as me.

Years after we sold it, I visited the house where I'd grown up. I thought I'd find the past intact and undisturbed, but I discovered the house was under reconstruction. I almost didn't recognize it.

    I had gone over in the early evening, after the workers had left. The late afternoon sun was playing on familiar surfaces in well-known patterns. Near the cellar door I found piles of wallboard and lath, and inside lay strips of our old wallpaper. The back door had obligingly been left open, and in a moment, I was standing in our living room. Except that it wasn't our living room anymore, just an empty rectangular space. None of the rooms contained any furniture. Paint cans and roller trays were scattered about, and my footsteps sounded unnatural and out of place. By ripping out the wood and plaster, the workers were excavating me, chipping away at my connection to the past, carting off piece by piece, the past itself.

The carpeting on the stairs had been removed, and the second floor stood as empty as the first. The walls had been stripped of paint and paper, and the fading rays of the sun stretched from room to room in the silvery winter light. The third floor was darker than the others, and strange shadows flickered through the air. When I was growing up, my father had spent a lot of time on that floor, doing reconstruction of his own. He spackled the ceiling, laid down carpeting, and installed several brass light fixtures.

Over a hundred years before we moved in, the house sat on a small farm and housed a few household servants. One of them, a young woman from Ireland, hanged herself from the rafters on the third floor. Even before my father told me about it, I avoided going to the up there. Maybe it was the darkness or its isolation from the rest of the house, but I never felt alone in those rooms. Some nights I even thought I heard voices whispering up and down the hallway.

As a child, I used to have nightmares about being held by invisible hands on that floor. I would steal from room to room looking for the stairs and never finding them. The walls would close in, doorways vanish, and suddenly I had no idea where I was. The dream always ended with me crashing headlong through a window; I'd fly over the roof, while splintered glass floated musically to the ground.

Most of the walls were gone now; wood scraps and nails

littered the floor. The work must have been recently done, maybe that day. Plaster dust hung in the air. Nothing resisted me as I penetrated to the other side of the missing wall. For a moment, reality was uncertain. I had become the ghost.

After my brother graduated high school and left home, I moved into his third floor room. I didn't feel completely at ease making that that space my own, but it was an opportunity I couldn't turn down. I would be a flight of stairs away from the second floor, where Tracy and my mother slept. Claudia was already at college in Pennsylvania, and the appeal of living in that apartment of sorts, where I would feel like an adult, was a beauty not lost on a teenage boy.

But in the course of a year, a few unusual things happened up there. I have never been a sleepwalker, but one morning I awoke in the guest room down the hall. I don't remember making that trip in the middle of the night; it had never happened before and would never happen again. Another morning, at dawn, I was suddenly awakened from a deep sleep. I sprung bolt upright in bed, pulling my pillow from behind my head and hurling it at the doorway. I saw a woman standing there looking at me.

The last time I ever saw my father, I decided to ask him about the third floor. I was curious whether he'd ever sensed anything unusual up there. I thought my asking about it would make him laugh and roll his eyes. My father claimed to be an atheist and would probably think it ridiculous to believe in anything invisible. But I never thought not believing in God meant one couldn't believe in spirits.

I had just turned 30 the last time I ever saw my father. It was a cold morning in October and he and I were sitting on the sofa together in his living room.

Dad," I said, "did you ever feel anything up there?"

He knew exactly what I meant and paused a moment before answering.

"Yeah, I felt it," he said evenly. He never said another word about it.

I wish I had asked him a few questions that day. I would love to know if he'd seen or heard anything strange in those rooms.

For me, the supernatural world is alive and well. But there's nothing paranormal about the kind of ghost that hides behind scenery flats in a high school auditorium. That ghost rises from the graveyard of memory, chapters fastened together to form an ongoing narrative. I don't want to get stuck on my earthly voyage, where time doesn't really pass. Being frozen like that is a ghostly existence, and I only want to revisit a few people and places and stay for a while. A disease is the ghost in the haunted house I know as my body.

CHAPTER 10

In the Jungle

Enclosure

I strayed into the zoo
and found all the enclosures ajar.
A lion slept on a wall,
her paws splayed wide as the moon.
The sky bled darkness
and echoed peals of a coming storm
that swallowed the world in shadow.
The lion approached me then,
quiet as the dawn,
and asked me in silence
to join her.

Around the time I went through my old house, I took a trip to the zoo and stopped at the tiger's cage. Two of them were lying against the back wall, as far from the people as they could get. The third paced back and forth just behind the iron bars. I admired these proud, mysterious creatures. They were no threat to those looking at them from outside their cage but might cause problems for someone stumbling upon one in the wild.

I was sure that if the cage doors suddenly opened, the tigers would escape in the blink of an eye. They would shoot up the embankment by the soda stand and disappear before the spectators had time to panic. To a tiger, freedom might matter more than almost anything. Their instincts are never wrong, and they are not easily fooled. When you strip any animal, including a human being, of its dignity, you'd be wise to restore it quickly.

Cats without a master have always ranked high among my favorite animals. I love their sleek beauty and quiet watchfulness. That day, I stood in front of the tiger cage for a long while. I looked into those unblinking yellow eyes that seemed not to see the bars, or the spectators, the shaded concrete walk with its wooden benches, or the clouds of colored balloons. Those eyes were staring somewhere else, taking in a different scene, one with no fences.

The tiger's compound was dotted with trees, and grass, and large blocks of granite where the animals could sun themselves and sleep their lives away in the static dream common to all imprisoned creatures. The zoo keepers could have believed that if the tiger compound looked like a natural habitat, the animals might have been fooled into thinking no crime was being committed against them. The same trickery is used to keep tropical fish happily distracted for the whole of their brief lives. If a parakeet can swing on a wooden perch, look at itself in the chip of a mirror, and ring a bell with its beak, why would it need to fly?

As it is to a tiger, freedom is extremely important to me. I'm unhappy to have lost a good deal of mine. I now encounter barriers in the most modest of forms—a low hill, a small stream—most of them not a problem even for a child. But they are significant hurdles for me and represent a world that is forever receding. Since the days my physical state of affairs began to decline noticeably, I've been envious of another creature's ability to move without assistance. You'll never see a lion in a wheelchair or a leopard pushing a walker.

Just after my visit to the zoo, I began having dreams that involved wild cats. One night, I dreamed I was back at the house where I grew up. It was a bright spring day, and I stood at the front door, holding a huge brass key ring, as though I were a zoo keeper myself. There were fifty keys on that ring. I tried one after another, but though every key fit, not one unlocked the door. I looked through the glass panel, thinking someone might be home. The house was unnaturally dark, as though the sunlight couldn't penetrate the windows. My father had recently left my mother, but when I peered in the window, I saw his suitcase sitting on the floor at the bottom of the stairs.

"It's night in there," I whispered to myself as I stepped back from the door. A moment later the forsythia bush shook and a leopard leapt out and landed nimbly on the railing behind me. I whirled around and saw him; the leopard was so close I could smell his fur. With another bound he landed at my feet. Before he moved past me, he looked into my eyes. It seemed as though he wanted me to follow him. Then he slipped by and disappeared through the door that now stood ajar. I trembled, afraid, not of the leopard, but of what my father might do if he found a leopard in the house. The leopard suddenly disappeared into the dark, the darkness he came from and embodied.

In another dream I had back then, I was alone in our house one day and sensed I was in danger of some kind. I raced downstairs and ran from room to room, locking all the doors. By the time I got to the back door, it was too late, a tiger stood there staring at me. I was terrified, but he didn't move. It seemed like he was waiting for me to invite him in.

A psychologist once wrote that people who dream about wild animals are repressing parts of themselves. I finally realized the cats in my dreams didn't represent my father: they symbolized the me I was hoping to become. The cats had qualities I didn't have, not in abundance. I wasn't proud that in my dreams I often cowered behind closed doors. I think the cats would have liked me to stand a little taller. They easily penetrated all the barriers I put between us, but they never attacked. It took me a long time to consider the possibility that they just wanted to play with me. I think they hoped to assure me that nothing could take away my dignity. The cats may have been merely an embodiment of my subconscious. Deep inside, I might have sensed a battle was coming and wanted a few allies in my camp.

CHAPTER 11

Iowa

Heat Lightning

This evening, again,
light dances on the horizon,
inviting me to try keeping step,
flaring the cumulous clouds,
like a candle sputtering
inside a white paper bag.
Every night comes the thunder,
but no lightning
and never a drop of rain.
The sky has become a tease,
promising relief with dark, swollen clouds,
but delivering nothing.
I've begun to worry
that the sky has forgotten how to rain,
like a man who has gone too long without crying.
I listen for the sound of leaves
lifting their silvery veins

in a promising wind.
I want to hear water tapping
on the roof over my head,
have been waiting weeks for deliverance,
staring at cracked and browning fields.
The sound of Nature rousing from sleep
keeps edging to the impossible;
only the crickets sing on, unconcerned,
for they can slake their thirst on a drop of dew
that hangs from a pale and dusty blade of grass.

I had planned to begin graduate school in September, but the seizure took the wind out of my sails. I decided to put off moving to the Midwest until the following January. One snowless, frigid Sunday evening in the first week of the year, the Greyhound bus I had ridden halfway across the country rolled into the center of Iowa City. We drove into a gas station and pulled into a parking space outside the visitor center; I climbed down the steps and entered the icy night air. I hurriedly carried my two suitcases into the building. That night, the temperature would drop to three degrees below zero. The frosty air caught in my lungs like a stone.

 I knew no one in that town, but my brother's wife had a friend who lived there with her husband and their two children. My brother had given me Jessica's phone number and told me to call her when I got to town. He thought it would be fine to ask Jessica for a ride to a motel. I took my brother's advice and dialed her number. Jessica answered in a friendly voice. I told her who I was and why I was calling.

"Where are you?" she very pleasantly asked.

"At the visitor center in town," I answered.

"Stay right there," she said. Jessica arrived ten minutes later with her two kids and set my suitcases in the trunk. I got into the passenger seat and shut the door.

"I really appreciate this," I said, smiling at her. "I'd be incredibly grateful if you could drive me to a motel. I'd like to sleep in a real bed tonight."

"Don't be ridiculous," she said as she pulled onto the street. "You're spending the night with us. That's Jason and Amanda," she said, hooking a thumb over her shoulder. "Ron, my husband will be home soon."

She turned and continued driving away from the town center. "So, where are you from?" Jessica asked. "I can't remember."

"New Jersey," I answered.

"Is this your first time in Iowa?"

"I flew over it once a few years ago," I told her.

"You flew back, didn't you?" I nodded. "So, you've been in Iowa twice."

"I guess," I said. "Sort of."

We smiled at each other.

I had dinner that night with Jessica, Ron and their kids.

"Where do you live?" Amanda said, studying me across the table.

"I'm trying to find something in town," I told her, smiling.

"I'm sure you'll find *something*," she said confidently.

"Yeah," said Jason, "but it might not be a place to live. Like, I found a blue jay feather yesterday."

Jessica walked around the table and switched on the stove.

"But I think he really wants to find a place to *live*," she told her son. Over dinner, I asked Jessica and Ron where they worked. Jessica told me she was a freelance graphic artist, and Ron told me he spent part of his days in an operating room at the university hospital. He was studying to become an anesthesiologist.

After dinner, the two of them got up.

"Why don't you sprawl out on the couch and relax," Ron said to me. "We're going downstairs to get your room ready for you."

"Oh, please don't go to any trouble," I said.

"It's no trouble at all," said Ron.

He and Jessica went downstairs, and I slid the newspaper off the kitchen counter. I sat down and started going through the classifieds, looking for an apartment or a house with rooms to rent. I found a listing for a two-story house near the university; it had four bedrooms, and one was available. I called the number listed and talked to one of the three tenants, a friendly guy named Greg. He was a graduate student in physics, studying for a PhD. We agreed to meet the next day.

In the morning, Jessica pulled up a chair beside me at the kitchen table and sat down. Amanda was sitting at the head of the table, looking at me intently. I looked back at her.

"Hi," I said. She rested a fist on her cheek and looked away.

"Are you going into town today?" she asked me, keeping her hand in place and tilted her head to the side.

"I'm going to look at a house," I told her. It seemed that Amanda was trying to figure me out.

"What if you're not *supposed to* live in a house," she said. "What if you're meant to live in a tree?" She was silent for a little while. Then she asked me another question: "Do squirrels live in trees? Do they even sleep? I've never seen one sleeping."

I began wondering if I'd make a good father. I'd thought about it a few times in the last several years and was usually pretty sure I'd be an improvement on my own father, but maybe I wouldn't. I had a feeling I'd never find out.

"Ron's off this morning," Jessica told me. "So, he'll stay here with the kids while we have a look at this place."

"What are you looking for, exactly?" Ron asked me from the sofa. "The closer you get to the university, the pricier places tend to be. But you can certainly find affordable housing all over. Just stay away from undergraduates. They can be real slobs. I sure was when I was in school."

Jessica and I left the house in a few minutes and got into the car.

We pulled out of the driveway and headed into town. In a few minutes she turned right and drove slowly down the street. "Here it is," she said, pulling up to the curb. "I'll wait for you."

I went to the front door and rang the bell. A minute later, the door was opened by a young woman in blue jeans and a corduroy jacket.

"Hi, I'm Margitt. Are you Keith?"

"I am," I said. "Is this the house that's looking for a roommate?"

"Ummm...houses can't really see. But, yeah, we're looking."

I liked her right away.

On my first day of classes at the University of Iowa Writers Workshop, where I went to hone my skills as an essayist, I went to my seminar on twentieth century English prose. The professor began calling the roll and getting acquainted with her students. "Sean Vernon," she said to the class.

"Here," I said. "But, could you please call me Keith? That's my middle name, but I've used it as my first name my entire life." I was thinking I'd probably have to make this request in every class.

"Not a problem," the professor replied. "Keith it is."

I thanked her and she moved down the roster. On my way to class two days later, I suddenly decided I would start using 'Sean' as my first name from that day on, rescuing it from the shadows where it had been hiding for over twenty-seven years. I'd never liked the name Keith and I could never understand why I was named Sean, which I thought a great name, and never called it. New start, new name.

When the professor ran down her roster again, she said, "Sean Ver—I'm sorry—*Keith* Vernon." She smiled at her mistake.

"I'm really sorry," I apologized, "but I've decided to start using my real first name. Can you please call me Sean?"

She smiled at me. I seemed to amuse her. "Will you be Sean from now on? Are you sure?" she asked.

"Absolutely," I said.

The day before the semester began, I signed up for an essay workshop run by Carl Klaus. I heard he was a brilliant teacher and very committed to his work, but that he had long been feisty and combative with his students. He used to intimidate them and made sure he always got the last word in any discussion; he seemed to think his word was the only one that mattered. One night all that changed. A few years before I met him, Klaus had been relaxing at home with his wife and started to belch a few times every minute. His wife quickly grew concerned and told him she wanted to drive him to the university hospital. In the emergency room, they told him he was having a heart attack. After they got him out of danger, the cardiologist told him that unless he eliminated stress from his life as much as possible, he probably wouldn't live a long one.

Overnight, Klaus became a different man and a different teacher. Although he was as passionate as ever about writers saying important things and saying them well, he actually started listening to his students. Still quick to defend his views and his understanding of the author's ideas, he slowed down and allowed others to speak their minds. "What do *you* think?" he would now ask his students, truly wanting to know. Though still spirited when expressing his views, he no longer dismissed another's ideas if they didn't agree with his. That was the Klaus I never knew, one I probably wouldn't have liked.

At the beginning of every class, one or two of us passed out copies of an essay we had written and wanted discussed. One day, I brought in copies of my latest essay and passed them around. I had written about an elderly woman who lived by herself at the edge of a large farm in the Midwest. One bitterly cold January morning, the woman stepped onto the side porch to pick up the morning paper. The kitchen door swung closed behind her and locked. She was only wearing a nightgown, a thin bathrobe and slippers. The temperature was five degrees above zero. When a neighbor found her the next day, she was slumped on the deck. She probably hadn't lasted very long.

'In this life,' I wrote, 'horrors come in all shapes and sizes. The losses awaiting each of us will have their own shades and dimensions. My personal demons may well throw a party in my honor, but I'd rather not attend.'

After everyone finished reading my essay, the students gathered their thoughts. Klaus glanced around the room.

"Do we all become fallen angels in the end?" he said.

I came to expect this sort of thing from him. My answers to his questions were never as interesting as having them wheeling around in my head. I never left his class with quite the same thoughts. Later, I would ask myself if I could ever rank as a fallen angel. Given my body's coming shenanigans, I'd have to learn to accept the first part, but I don't think I'll ever qualify for a magical being.

I met Hilary at the beginning of April, a few months later. One day I was walking into town with Margitt, my new housemate. As we passed a three-story office building, a man came out wearing a dress shirt, gray slacks, and brown wing-tip shoes.

Hilary!" Margitt called out. "What the heck are you up to? I haven't seen you in centuries!"

"I don't think it's been *that* long," Hilary said, smiling at her. "I'm pretty sure it's only been a few weeks. That's not even *half* a century!"

"This is Sean," Margitt told him. "He's in grad school here, too."

Hilary looked at me then back to Margitt. "You want to get some Chinese food?" he asked us. "It's really good. And fairly cheap."

At lunch that day, Hilary asked me where I was from.

"New Jersey," I answered. "A town called Madison."

"Are you serious?" he asked me. "That's unbelievable; I'm from Millburn, just down the road."

"We always lost to Millburn in football," I told him. "We hated you guys."

"Yeah, we didn't think much of you either." We both laughed.

Hilary was in his second year of graduate school, on his way to receiving a PhD in English Literature. A couple years older, he was tall and thin, like me. We had both grown up dangerously sensitive. Dangerous for us, not for others. A friend once called me weird, which I took as a compliment. I'm convinced Hilary would have felt the same way. Being thought of as weird made us both smile.

One summer evening, Hilary walked to the park to meet up with me and play a game we had both loved since we were kids. Hilary was carrying his Whiffle ball and the official plastic bat. I brought out the kid in Hilary, and he did the same for me. Standing in the grass under the stars, we pitched, slashed at the ball, ran the imaginary bases, and had fun in our adult-size sneakers, our heads blissfully free of adult-sized concerns. Like most children, Hilary and I each had complicated relationships with our mothers. We knew what made them happy, and we routinely fell short of the mark in that department.

After Hilary and I finished our first year we each returned home to New Jersey. At noon one Saturday, about two weeks after getting back from Iowa City, I walked up the steps of a large, white clapboard house where he'd grown up.

That day, I watched Hilary attend to his mother's every need while the three of us sat at her kitchen table. To stay on top of the never-ending demands required Hilary to pay careful attention to anything that could upset the rickety apple cart beside him. He sat in the chair next to his mother while she reclined in her wheelchair and barked orders at him. He had to prepare her toast, make her a cup of tea, clean the kitchen counter, the list was endless. It seemed he was required to stay out of her way while fulfilling her every whim.

When he led me through the house and all those echoing rooms padded with dust, I thought at once of Miss Saltus; both houses were places of vast loneliness stretching back through the years. The houses reminded me of the tour I had taken of my own childhood home. Hilary and I climbed the stairs at his house to the second floor. The locked bedroom door at the head of the stairs made me a little nervous. It was the room where Hilary's father had slept and where he hid from his wife, for reasons Hilary didn't want to discuss. The door was gouged and scratched, as though something had repeatedly tried to claw its way in.

"They're my mother's marks," Hilary told me, though he didn't really have to. He pointed out the spittle that had stuck to the panel and hardened there. Petrified venom. My mother and father battled somewhat at times, but they never approached this kind of intensity. Still, I felt strangely at home in Hilary's house. And suddenly, I saw that Hilary and I were more alike than I had realized.

In Hilary, I saw what looked like blind devotion to the past, which he covered up with humor and cynical poses. I left him abruptly that day, having grown afraid of what other nightmarish details I might discover in that house. I could spend time tending to my own skeletons instead. Perhaps because he'd grown up in a battle zone, Hilary had little faith in having a bright future, which would have explained his resistance to making plans, and his panicky sense of not having enough time. It made him a bit of a recluse, something else we had in common. I was always afraid to approach him in public, worried that I'd be intruding, and taking away precious minutes he could never get back.

Hilary even had the complexion of a ghost, pale and a little indistinct. In Iowa, he left his phone unplugged for weeks at a time. Someone who couldn't reach him by telephone might have concluded he had moved away. I sometimes worried that he had abandoned important parts of himself. I wondered if I'd done the same thing. Hilary's house in Iowa City looked deserted. Some nights I would drive by and see the windows gleaming behind the pine trees. I'd occasionally call him a few hours later, but he seldom answered the phone. I wondered if Hilary disconnected it to ward off visitations from his mother. The telephone was the only route to him his mother had left. But it didn't matter; Hilary couldn't keep memories of his past out. I've found that I can't keep the past away either. I came to see Hilary as a sad-eyed, wounded man nursing a deeply buried grief. Almost from the day I met him, I felt we came from the same home.

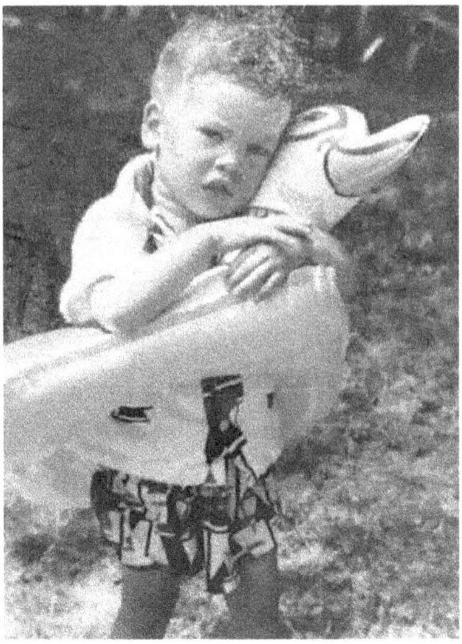
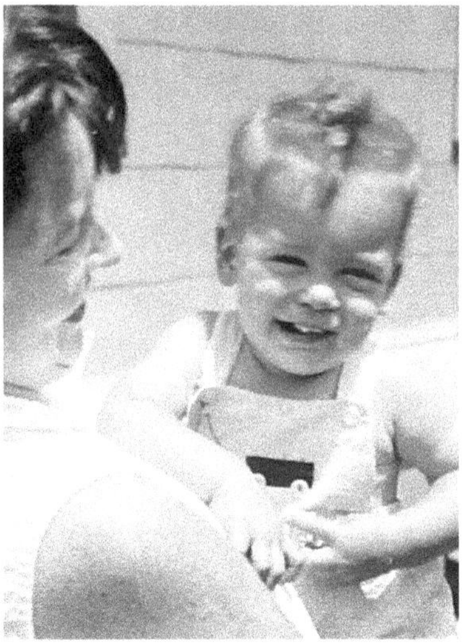
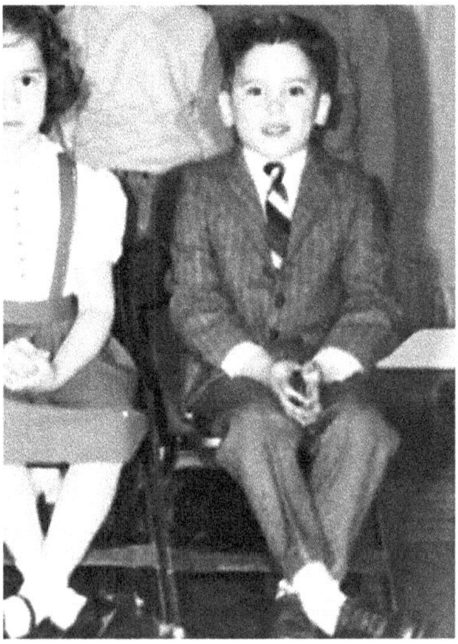
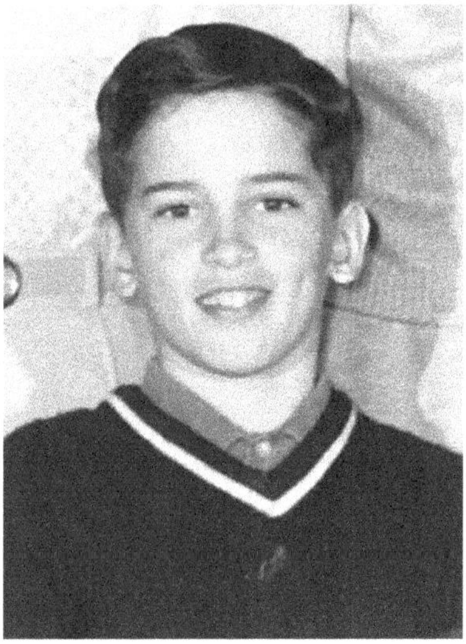

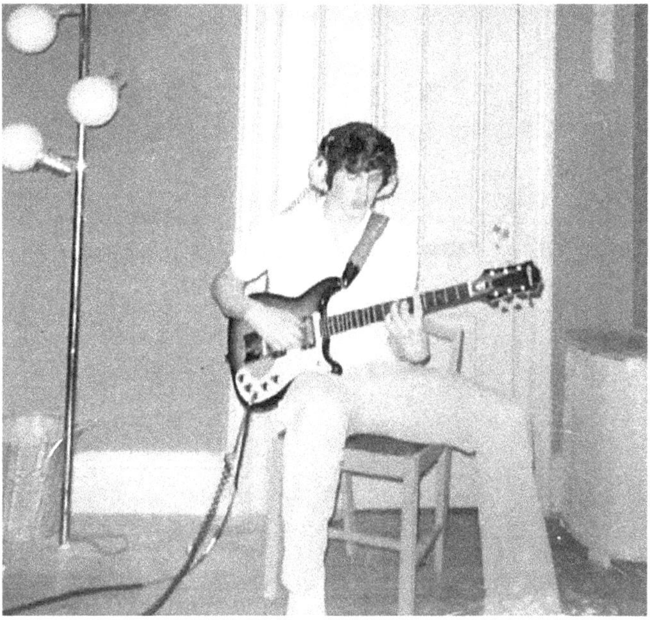

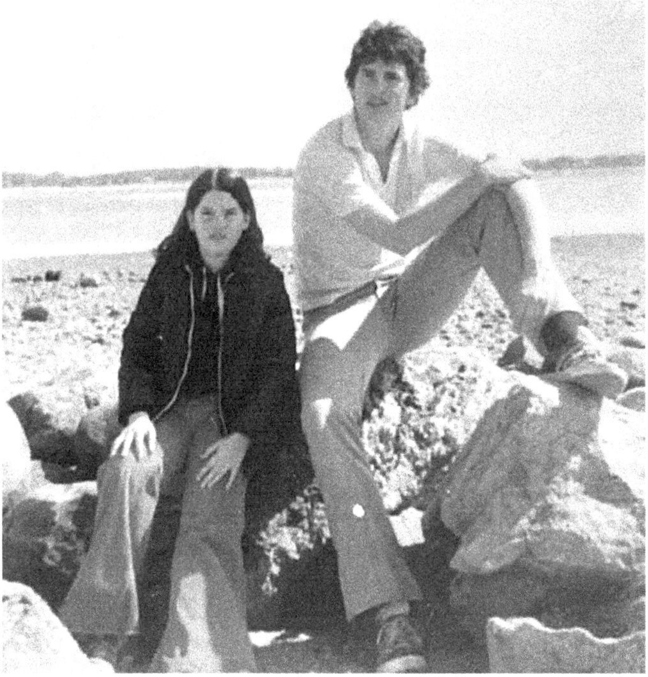

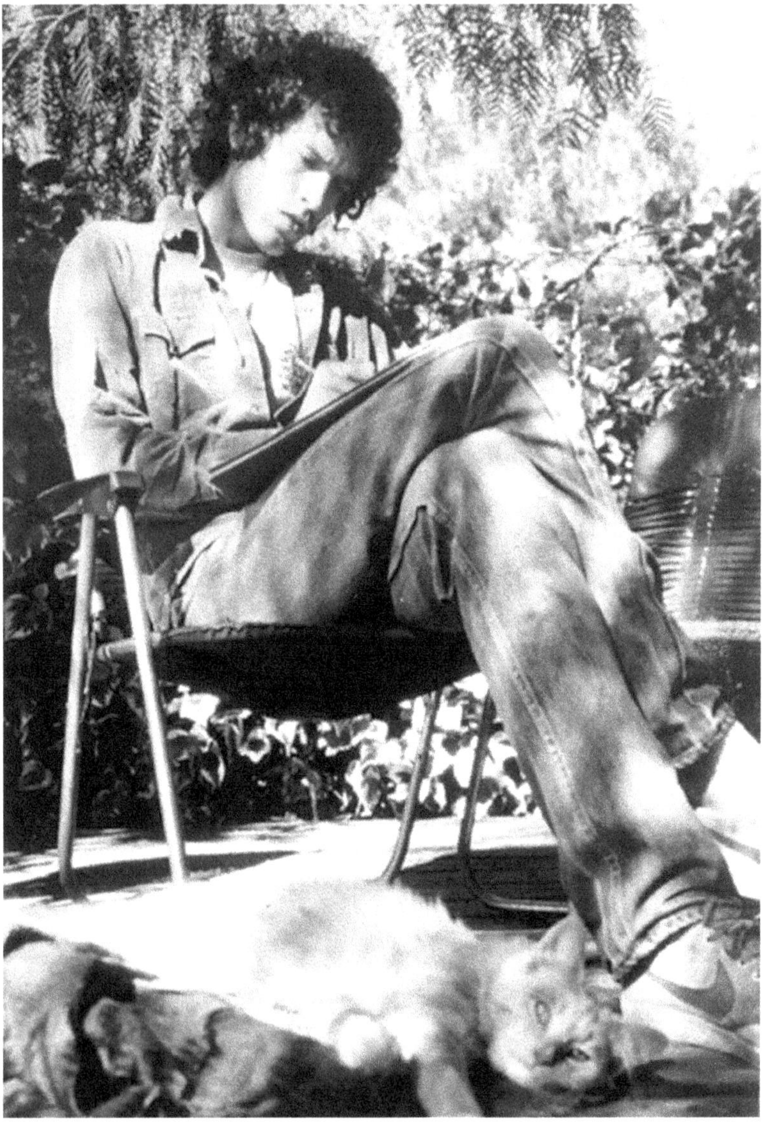

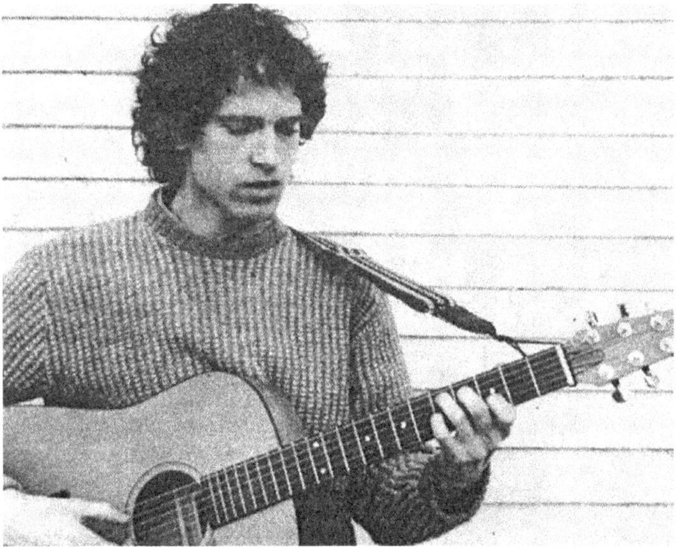

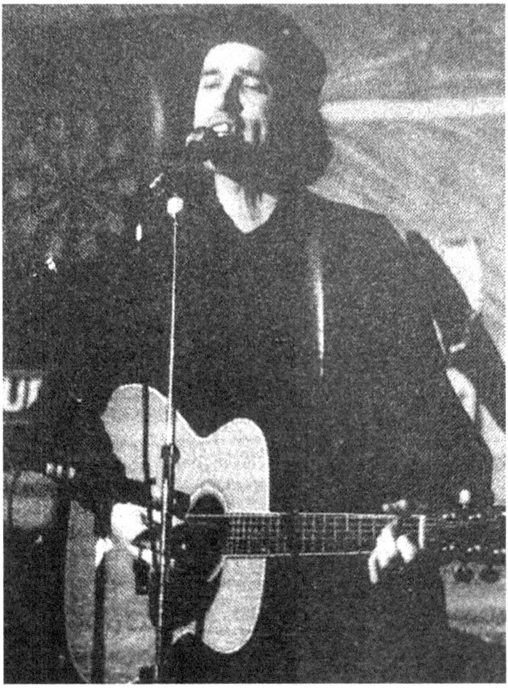

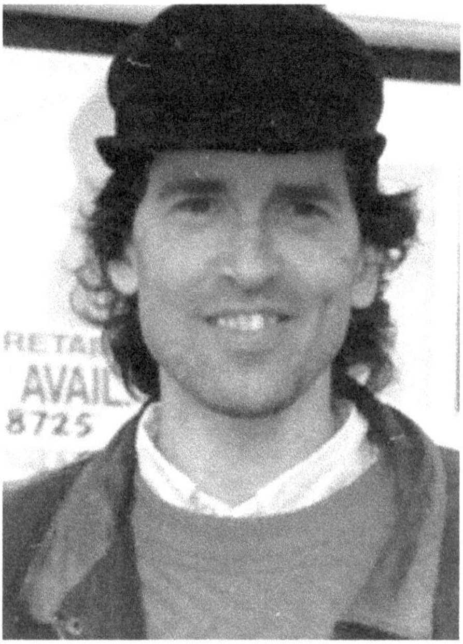
RETAI
AVAIL
8725

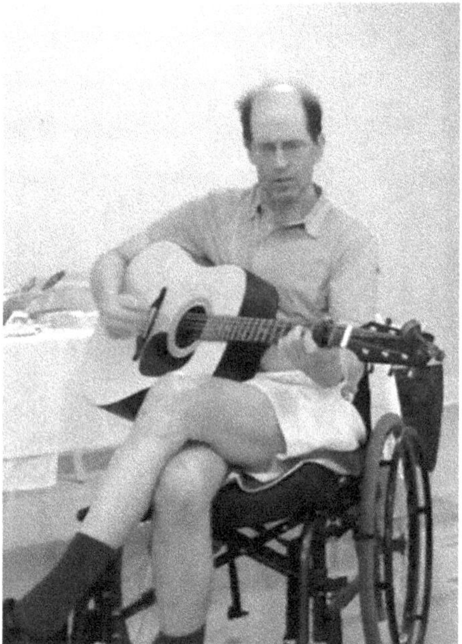

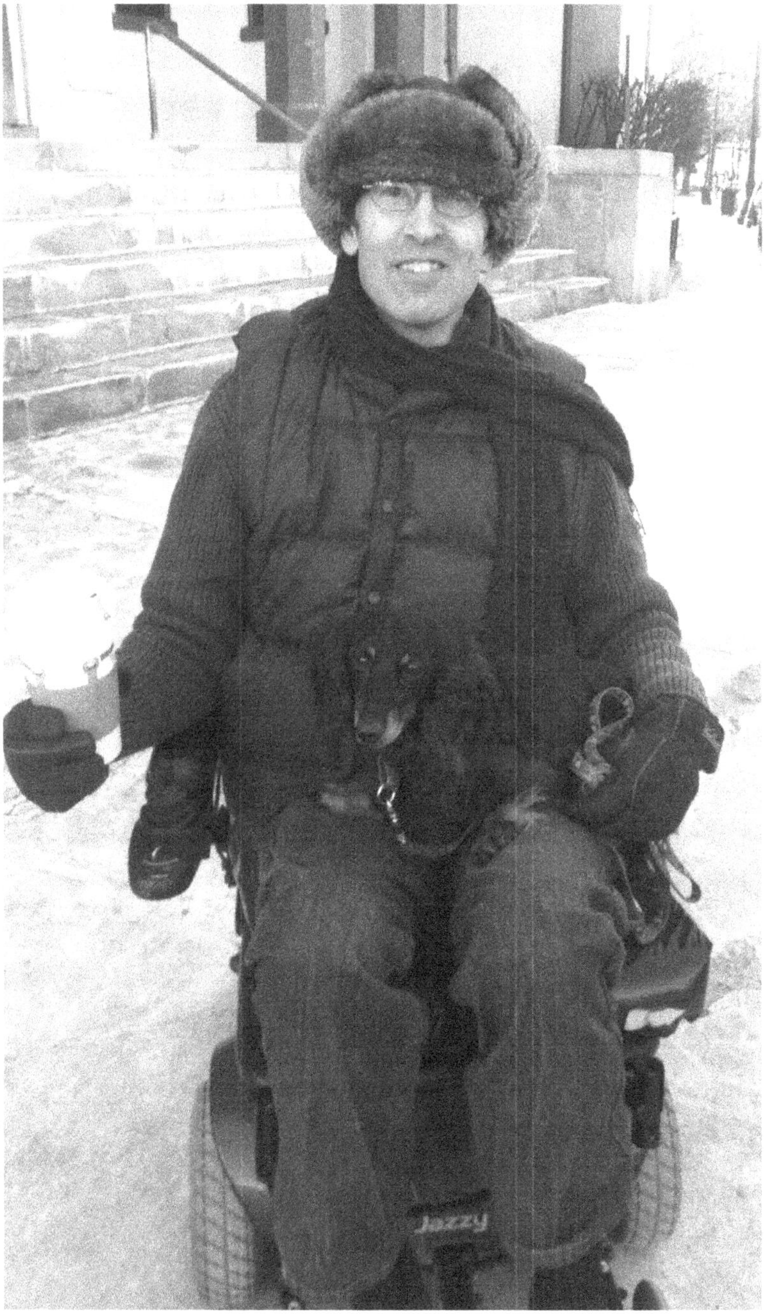
Jazzy

CHAPTER 12

Denial is Not a River

Where Does The Rainbow End?

Where does the rainbow end?
maybe in a place very much like this,
with no sound but the far-off drone
of a ghostly transport.
The future never looked so much like the past,
moral bearings eclipsed,
reason blown away like smoke,
my heart losing blood and growing cold.
Fear has come home;
it has maneuvered the tides,
darkened the heavens,
and hidden the way to your door,
behind which lies the museum of your sitting room,
the crypt of you bed,
and the nostalgia of sweat,
the bumping into walls in the blindness of night
the clues of infidelities surrounding us like fog,

unfamiliar clothing that was never returned,

the omissions,

the lies,

the grey cat with yellow eyes.

who sat on the sill and watched.

Color fades like a dream past resurrection,

sinking beneath the waves

obscured by the refraction

of a world utterly changed

and moving no one knows where.

After my first year in Iowa City, I moved out of my first house and relocated to a four room, second floor apartment and lived with a thirty-year-old guy named Tom. He was doing a PhD in what he called the "beautiful dead end of philosophy." In his free time, Tom sang bluegrass songs, accompanying himself nicely on guitar. He was a pretty good songwriter. He taught me a lot of old folk and bluegrass tunes

Tom and I traded songs every day. Earlier that week, I'd been sitting in the living room, guitar in hand, working on a setting of *Fear no More the Heat o' the Sun* from Shakespeare's *Cymbeline. (Fear no more the frown of the great/ Thou art past the tyrant's stroke.)* Tom looked in on his way down the hall and listened for a minute.

"What's that?" he asked, when I noticed him and stopped playing.

"I'm setting something by Shakespeare."

"Your music?" he said.

"Yeah. It doesn't sound like anything, does it?" I always wanted to be sure a song I was writing hadn't already been written.

"I don't think so," he said. "No, I never heard that melody. It's nice." With that, he turned and walked out. I don't think my music was to his taste, but, with very few exceptions, Tom always applauded anyone writing a song.

One sunny day in late spring, I was walking across a campus lawn toward the Iowa River. About twenty yards from the grassy riverbank stood a tiny brick chapel. I wasn't even sure it *was* a chapel: I never saw anyone inside or heard church bells chiming. That day, I decided to get a closer look. I strode up the walkway to the door and around to the side of the building. Standing before a line of small windows, I looked through the glass, and saw several pews sat at the center of the space before a small wooden podium. A few months before, I had been thinking of giving a concert, and performing some of my musical settings of well-known poems. This seemed an ideal place.

The next day, I called the activities department at the University and spoke to a woman named Evelyn. I asked her if the chapel was ever used for things besides religious services.

"It's used a lot for weddings," she said. "Are you getting married?"

"I'm not," I said. "I want to use it for a little concert I'm planning. I'd play some of my musical settings of poems."

"It would be a great place for that," she said. "Are these poems students read in class?"

"A lot of them are," I said.

"Good. I can't deal with a lot of the new ones. My teenage

son writes poems, but I have no idea what they're about. I told him that once, and it made him happy. He says that if people understand a poem of his, it's not a good poem. I don't know. If you don't want people to understand what you've written, why write?" She laughed a little. "So, how many people are you expecting at your event?"

"I don't really know. I figure if I don't expect anyone, I won't be disappointed."

"I hear you," she said. "But it can be very hard to not expect things. If you figure out how to do that, be sure to let me know."

Evelyn told me the chapel would comfortably seat about thirty people. The night of my little concert, eleven people showed up, and that was just fine with me. I didn't know if anyone would show.

I was sitting in a chair by the door and watched the audience straggle in. I recognized a few faces. One of the first people to arrive was a man from my essay workshop. I'd never talked to him, but I admired his writing.

Sitting a little way down the pew was a man I often saw in a café downtown. He always carried in a brown leather journal and wore a tie. I wondered what he was writing: A novel? A philosophical treatise? His autobiography?

A young woman entered by herself and took a seat in the last row. I had seen her a few times in the building that housed most of the school's literature classes and the writing workshops. I once saw her present some of her poetry at a reading in a downtown cafe. I loved the musical lilt of her voice and the rhythms of the words. Her poems were passionate and haunting.

In a few minutes people stopped coming into the chapel. I got up, lifted my guitar off the stand, and looked at the small gathering before me. I had almost never played my settings for an audience of more than one or two people, and I was a little nervous. But only a little. Much as I felt happy and at peace in Iowa, I knew I wouldn't be putting roots down in this part of the country, and that helped me relax. The audience's reaction didn't really matter to me. I knew I'd probably never see these people again. At least, I was almost sure I wouldn't.

"Thank you all for coming," I said. "Tonight, I'm going to join two of my favorite things: music and poetry. Songwriters, a select few of them, have been combining these for a long time. Tonight I'm going to play you a few of my musical settings of poems by Shakespeare, W. B. Yeats, Christina Rossetti, Langston Hughes, and a few others. The first one is a poem by one of my very favorite poets, Emily Dickinson. She's telling us what she would have to do to feel she hasn't lived in vain." Then I played them my setting of this poem:

If I can stop one Heart from breaking
I shall not live in vain
If I can ease one Life the Aching
Or cool one Pain
Or help one fainting Robin
Unto his Nest again
I shall not live in vain.

For me to feel I haven't lived in vain, it would be enough to have spent that hour in the chapel on the banks of the Iowa River.

*

One night we were sitting in the living room playing songs together. Tom was singing the old Merle Travis song, *Dark As A Dungeon: Oh come all you young fellers so young and so fine/ And seek not your fortune in a dark dreary mine.*

Suddenly the doorbell rang. Tom's friend, Jessica, had stopped in for a visit with a friend, a pretty young woman named Josie. They came in and sat down on a couple of living room chairs. I recognized her immediately as the poet from my concert, and thanked for coming to it.

"So you're in the poetry workshop here?" I asked.

"Yes, I'm working on a book of poems." She said.

"I could use the help of a poet," I told her. "I need words to go with a melody I've written. I asked a few people in the workshop to give it a shot. Three or four of them wrote something, but I wasn't happy with any of it. Can a person who writes poetry write good lyrics?"

"They're pretty much the same thing," Josie said.

"You're probably right. Will you give it a try?"

"Sure, I need to hear what you've written, though."

I got out my guitar and fingerpicked the chords, humming the melody as I played. While she was listening, Josie took out a pen and a piece of paper and scribbled something. When I finished, she folded it up and put it in her pocket.

After breakfast the next morning, I went downstairs to head for the campus. In the mailbox, a piece of paper was sticking out. I removed it and saw the words she'd written for my melody.

Restless lady

Restless lady
Sleep through your sorrow
Spring is made for full-blown roses
Sweeter than you

Breathe soft, breathe slow
Broken and voiceless
Night is made for silver rainstorms
Wilder than you

Light on your pillow like fire
River of dreams and desire
No one drowns inside of sleep

You sleep through midnight
Still all the memories
Eternity is meant for diamonds
Harder than you.

When I got back from school a few hours later, I pulled out my guitar, and sang her words to my melody. And that's how we began.

Josie lived on the second and third floors of a house several blocks from mine. In very short order, I realized that she was an unusual woman and a gifted writer. Although she had many friends, she kept to herself a few hours every day to write. Because of her, poetry opened its doors to me. She made me see that poetry needed to be read differently from prose, with greater attention to language and its rhythms. She showed me that poetry doesn't yield all its significance quickly, and in some cases never does. In time, I would see Josie as a poem, one that carried me into deep waters.

That summer, when I'd been living in Iowa for a year, Josie and I drove to Grenadier Island, in the St. Lawrence River. We were staying in a rambling 150 year-old house that belonged to the parents of David, a friend of Josie's. We greeted him at a dock on the St. Lawrence, and stepped into his yellow motorboat. We crossed the quarter mile of water to the opposite shore, got out of the boat, and walked up the grassy slope to the house. The paint on the outside walls was peeling and a number of the discolored floorboards on the front porch creaked when stepped on. Inside, all the rooms were dusty, the furniture antiquated, and every sound muffled. The house seemed abandoned and forgotten. I felt like a ghost passing through those rooms. The first-floor bedroom where Josie and I would sleep had three windows that afforded us a view of the front lawn. Josie asked me if I liked the island.

"I like having a river between me and civilization," I answered.

She looked at me and smiled. "You'll get no argument from me," she said. "I've long considered civilization overrated."

One afternoon I went off by myself and followed the trail to where David said there'd be a canoe tied to a tree on the shore.

"I have no idea who the boat belongs to," he said. "I don't think there's anyone around who'd notice if you take it for a spin."

I walked the trail for half a mile, ignoring the strange new feelings of tingling in my arms, and came to the spot where the canoe was tied to a sapling at the water's edge. A minute later, I was seated in the canoe and began paddling away from the shore and taking in the lovely scene around me. It was suddenly difficult to hold the paddle and I shook my arm to try to rid myself of the unusual sensation. I focused on the scenery. Trees with deep green leaves rocked slightly back and forth in the gentle wind. Delicate blue flowers peeked from the grass on the bank, as a raft of ducks floated around me in a tight circle some distance away.

I reached my arm into the water to check the temperature and leaned sideways further than I intended. With the numbness I was experiencing I had trouble righting myself and the boat tipped over and I plunged into the water. The creek began to fill the canoe. My only thought was that I had to prevent the boat from sinking. I grabbed the rope and tugged on it, wresting the canoe to shore. Not being a strong swimmer, and feeling somewhat anxious about my symptoms, the thought that I might drown shot through my mind. I tugged on the rope as hard as I could, and finally felt silt under my feet and knew I was safe.

That weekend on Grenadier Island was when the first wave of denial hit me. I had experienced puzzling, temporary physical conditions, such as numb patches on my forearm, fuzzy vision, difficulty enunciating and the tingling sensation, which I chose to ignore. A few weeks later, back in Iowa City, the disconcerting symptoms had disappeared. My denial was justified.

But then one day out of the blue, my vision went blurry. It didn't last long, but long enough to concern me. The symptoms were adding up and I couldn't get them out of my mind. Long ago I had recognized myself as a hypochondriac, but there was something different about these signs. I had no idea what they indicated: a series of mild strokes, an unusually belated aftershock of polio, which I'd never had—but I suspected they were clues of something disturbing. One day, I ventured into the town library and looked for a medical book on the symptoms of common diseases. I leafed through one and came to a section on multiple sclerosis. I ran down the list of symptoms, and I was certain I had it. The next day I made an appointment with a specialist at an MS clinic in Chicago.

At dinner that night, I told Josie of my discovery.

"You do know you're something of a hypochondriac, don't you?" Josie asked me. "Couldn't you be embellishing a little?"

"A hypochondriac isn't always wrong," I responded.

At my appointment with the neurologist a few weeks later, I described my recent symptoms for him. He performed a brief neurological exam, looking at my eyes, testing the strength of my hands, my arms, and legs. He had me touch the tip of his index finger with mine as he moved his hand around.

Finally, he sat back in his chair. "I see no sign of MS," he said. Then he looked over my biographical sheet. "You're about to finish grad school," he said, looking up at me. "I think you're just experiencing a lot of stress."

A minute later, Josie and I walked out of his office.

"See, you are a hypo."

I didn't tell her what I thought, but I knew the doctor was wrong. I was sure of it. Was this just my hypochondriacal thinking? Josie had entered the slippery world of denial and I decided to rejoin her in it.

The strange feelings, tinglings, numbness and weird vision came and went, and I decided to do nothing about them. Denial was sweet.

That year Josie and I left Iowa and resettled on the edge of a college town in New England. We were drawn there by the beauty of the area and its artistic and culturally rich environment. I loved Iowa, its unhurried pace, the trustworthiness of the people, its endless corn fields and long winding country roads that seemed in no hurry to end. But the East was calling me home. Tracy, my sister, had been living in that area for several years, having gotten a Bachelor's degree in dance at one of the nearby universities.

Once there, we scanned the classifieds in the local papers, looking for a place to live. We found one in a small hamlet twenty minutes from Amherst. The two-story clapboard house sat on a small town square and seemed ideal for us. There was a newly married young couple living there, and though they weren't likely to become close friends, they were polite and kept to themselves. In about a week, Josie and I had both found jobs to cover the rent. Josie found a position in a bookstore in a nearby town, and I took a temp job at a bank. I sat at a desk seven and a half hours a day, filing bank forms having to do with mortgages, personal loans, and all kinds of dreadfully uninteresting bank products. I was polite to the five women who worked there, and listened to them talk about their lives. To keep myself from being swallowed by waves of boredom, I secretly wrote poems and song lyrics. I wrote one for the women I worked with called 'The Ladies At The Bank.'

The Ladies At The Bank

The ladies at the bank complain from eight to four,
rude customers, the coffees muddy water,
and every year their benefits cost more.
The toffee and the rich crumb cake with butter,
that must be what they keep returning for.
Oh ladies, gentle ladies,
I know the bank mistreats you,
but it's your willingness to let it that defeats you.
Why not look for something better?
I'll even help you write the letter—
No one should have to do the work that you do.

The ladies at the bank are bored beyond belief;
their monotonous routines are stupefying.
The only way they seem to get relief,
is to talk about who's dead,
and who they know that's dying,
and for accuracy's sake they're never brief.
Oh my dear fluorescent ladies,
look what the bank has made you,
but the bank, all by itself cannot degrade you;
the men's offices are sunny,
the men make all the money,
and they don't do one half the work that you do.

The ladies at the bank arrive for work at eight,
not 8:02 or 7:57;
in over twenty years they've never once been late.
And when they die, they'll punch in on time in heaven,
applying blue eye shadow at the gate.

One afternoon, I was sitting at my desk and got hit by the idea that Josie was being unfaithful. I didn't know where the notion came from; she had never seemed unhappy or distant with me. I sat there at my desk wondering where this feeling in the pit of stomach was coming from. Then I remembered the party we had gone to a few weeks before. I had noticed a penetrating look passing between her and some guy at the party. As usual, I ignored it and never mentioned it when we got home. But I *knew* it. It would have been easy to add this denial to my long list. Something like self-preservation took over. I went to my supervisor and told her I wasn't feeling well and needed to go home. When I reached the house, I found that Josie wasn't there. I went inside and climbed the stairs to our room. I sat on our bed and waited. Josie's car rumbled into the driveway a half hour later. She walked through the front door and closed it behind her. She climbed the stairs and I half expected to hear footsteps following her. She walked alone into our bedroom. She was surprised to find me sitting there and just looked at me. I said nothing for a moment.

In a few seconds I spoke. "Why?"

"Because you thought I would," she replied simply. She seemed to have been expecting the question.

Actually, I hadn't planned to ask it, but what happened next is important. Nothing at all happened. I didn't even raise my voice to her.

And then, like my mysterious symptoms, I ignored it. Over and over again.

After about a year of it, I called my brother and told him what was happening. "I've got to get out of here," I said. "Could you help me move?"

"Of course," he said. "When are you planning to leave? I'll come up and do whatever you need. Except strangle her." But hurting her was the last thing on my mind. I was better at hurting myself. Maybe I was changing a bit. This decision was actually healthy.

About a year after Josie and I split up, I was having a cup of tea with a friend in a small café just up the street from the bookstore where Josie used to work. He had been the manager of that bookstore. He asked me if I believed in hell.

"I'm not sure," I said. "Why?"

"Because you were living in it with Josie," he said. "How did you stand it? She's a major tease!"

I was probably aware of that on a subterranean level, but when it came to Josie, I lived mostly on the denial side of the street. When I left the café and was walking home, I remembered the summer day I was strolling up Main Street when I noticed an attractive young woman walking in my direction. She stood out from the people around her. She wore a tight skirt cut halfway up her thigh and knee-high boots. There was something electric about her. "Do we have sex-workers in this town?" I remember thinking. Then I realized it was Josie. I quickly ducked down a side street and hurried away. I didn't want to remember Josie's ability to raise men's blood pressure.

Refusing to acknowledge unpleasantness of any kind has long been one of my coping strategies. I would soon be spending a lot of time with it. This particular practice helped me look the other way when things started to go seriously wrong with my body.

Somewhere in our first month together, Josie drove me to the western part of Iowa to meet her parents and see where she grew up. Upon entering the kitchen, I saw that her mother suffered from a kind of starvation anxiety. The kitchen cupboards were bursting with supplies. I opened a door and found nearly every variety of canned fruit. I lifted my head and discovered rows of canned soup, boxes of cereal, dried fruit in sealed plastic containers, and jars of assorted nut butters.

Josie stockpiled *men* to prevent a different kind of shortage. The arbiter of security was capturing men's attention. I wondered what had pulled me toward Josie, a woman who seemed likely to mangle my heart. Not given to expecting the worst of people, I proved an easy mark for her. People who serve tasty, probably unhealthy meals are often the ones I'm drawn to.

After Josie and I broke up, I realized it was high time I found a better place to live, a home furnished with a healthy self-interest. Like anyone, I needed a life in which my own physical and mental health were a priority, sometimes they hadn't been for me before. As symptoms slowly recurred, I suspected I had a real disease, and as it was knocking at the door, I would finally understand the love I needed most was my own.

CHAPTER 13

Cinema

Body

I am angry with you today;
you're not just anyone's,
and there are many days I wish you weren't mine.
I can't help but remember our beginning:
I used to roam the summer fields
watching my shadow sail across the grass
under the blue floor of heaven,
infinity laid out before me
in numberless shades of green.
I cover distance now
by telephone wire and the circuitry of memory.
When we fell into step, I didn't hear his foot fall,
as he quietly went to work, patient as death,
I didn't feel the earth shake
or see the water gathering itself beneath a calm surface.
I hate that my shoe-strings are now tied double,
by something working in the dark

teaching me the pocket of sunlight I lived in,
was temporary as peace on a battlefield.
I long for the stars to return,
and make this bandaged knot in my heart fall away,
letting me walk without dripping grief.

It was a Friday afternoon in July, and I'd just left the publishing company where I worked. I drove the few miles home and pulled into my driveway in the town where I lived with Tracy. I parked and got out of my blue Chevy Nova—a Spanish word that means "doesn't go." I liked the irony of that.

    I climbed the outside stairs to the second-floor apartment Tracy and I shared. I walked to my bedroom, threw my jacket and tie on the bed, and changed into a bathing suit, T-shirt, and sandals. I was looking forward to swimming in the nearby pond. I did it a couple times most weeks in the summer. The icy water bubbled up from an underground spring; the water temperature prevented some people from wading in further than a few feet from shore. It caused others to sit in the sand and soak up the rays of the sun. The water temperature didn't bother the children, they would have splashed around had there been ice cubes floating on the surface. I liked to defy fate by swimming across the pond. It wasn't more than 20 yards, but it wouldn't take more than a few seconds for a seizure to set in. The middle of a pond is not a great place to be when a seizure takes hold. But neither is a pool. Or a bathtub. For me, being in the water might have been bravery, foolishness, or denial. Not one was a stranger to me. I've always adored swimming. I once heard Nanny say that. And

I used to feel being in the water was something I couldn't live without. One thing this disease has taught me is that there are a good many things I can pretty easily live without. Discovering what they are has been an ongoing process for me.

I was on my way out the front door when I noticed the red light blinking on my answering machine.

"Dammit!" I snarled as I turned around. I didn't want anything to hold me up from diving into that water. But I thought it might be important, so I stepped to the shelf and impatiently pressed the button.

"Hello, Sean, this is Dr. Silver. Your MRI came back, and it showed lesions on the brain. So, as I suspected, you have MS. Come in next week and we'll talk about where we go from here." The machine clicked off.

I stood there for a few minutes in stunned silence. Then I walked to the bedroom, took off my bathing suit, and stepped into a pair of shorts. I didn't feel like swimming anymore. I just wanted to get into my car and drive. As I approached the front door, I looked to the left and saw my two cats sleeping on the bed. The message wouldn't have made the slightest difference to them. They didn't speak my language. I often envy an animal's partial oblivion.

I drove to the mall wanting to lose myself in front of the silver screen. After buying a ticket to the movie, I walked to a nearly empty theater and sat down in the last row. I have no idea what the film was called or what it was about. I just sat in the darkness and watched. The movie never really got my full attention. My mind kept drifting to memories of my trip to the hospital the day before. The symptoms had returned enforce and I knew I couldn't turn away any longer. Life was getting difficult. My doctor had been urging me to get an MRI.

I made the appointment without even knowing what an MRI was. I knew the machine didn't use radiation to capture its images. And I knew the letters stood for Magnetic Resonance Imaging. But what *that* was I couldn't say. I never really looked into it. I wasn't truly interested in learning about the technology. I knew it gave better pictures than the CAT Scan. The most important thing to me, is the machine had taken the best pictures of my brain I could get. What I didn't know was how it also tests your claustrophobia threshold and your ability to maintain a grip on reality, whatever the hell that is.

In the MRI room, I lay on a narrow table at the edge of a huge metal tube. The technician fitted my head snugly into a padded, doughnut-type thing. The technician handed me a pair of earplugs.

"Put these in," she said.

"Is this going to be very loud?" I asked her.

"Very. I'm going to slide you into the machine now," she said. "The noises are going to start right after you get in there. So put them in. Good luck. You'll do fine."

"Do some people not do fine?" I asked, a little concerned.

She just smiled. "You're going to be great! If you want to talk to us, push the red button on that console beside you."

She slid me headfirst into a long tube which completely engulfed me and was maybe three and a half feet in diameter. Then she turned and was gone. Alone in the tube, right away I started feeling like I wanted out. It's the same feeling I get when I'm sitting in a plane and the exit doors close.

I was lying there, my hands clasped, resting on my stomach wondering what the noise would be like when suddenly it started — an electronic THUD, low and deep and throbbing, as if the machine were coming to life. This happened a few times, then I heard nothing. The silence continued for several seconds. 'This isn't so bad,' I thought to myself. I felt relieved and wondered how long the test would take. I was afraid I might get a little bored. I was not so lucky. After a moment, a garbled male voice came through the speaker, "they're going to get faster now and a little louder." The interval between throbs was cut to half a second. It was as though a recording of a kid playing paddle ball was being fed through a synthesizer, and turned up very loud. I concentrated on the sound, trying to analyze it to remove myself from the whole experience, but it was too loud, too insistent. It was everywhere. Bouncing off the walls of the tube, bouncing off the walls of my skull. I closed my eyes, tried to imagine myself somewhere else, but I couldn't escape the wall of crazy sound. I wanted to move. I wanted to jump off the table, but then I'd just have to start all over again unless, of course I refused. I could just put on my clothes and walk out of there.

Suddenly silence. My whole body relaxed. It's over, I thought. I listened for the door opening, the technician's footsteps. Instead, I heard the garbled voice again, "Faster now, six minutes. You're almost through. And remember, don't move. We're getting great pictures."

This time they were maybe 10 beats to a second. Immediately, I started counting down... 59, 58, 57, 56, six times around and it would be over. I was into my second minute when the panic started rising. I opened my eyes, closed them, opened them again. It felt like my brain was buzzing, humming, about to explode.

When the torture was finally over, the silence was strange, but very welcome.

The technician came back and pulled me out. "How was it?" she asked.

"Can't you get some thicker earplugs?" I left as quickly as I could.

I was back in my body, in front of the movie screen. But it wasn't the same body. The MRI had made that clear.

After the film's final credits ended, I pushed through the doors of the theater and began wandering blankly down the hall to watch another forgettable film. After it ended, I left the mall, walked to my car and drove home. I parked in the driveway, next to Tracy's car, and mounted the stairs to our apartment.

Tracy was sitting on the sofa with her new boyfriend. I flopped into a chair on the other side of the room and looked at them.

"Hi," Tracy said brightly. She looked at the man beside her. "This is Carl."

"Hi," he said.

"Hi," I returned. Then I faced my sister. "I had an MRI yesterday, and today my doctor called and left me a fucking message—on a Friday no less! It seems I have MS."

For several seconds nobody spoke. No one knew what to say. I wondered if Tracy was running down a list of mysterious symptoms of her own.

"I've been having this weird numbness in my fingers," she said. "I wonder if *I* have MS?!"

"Of course you don't," I replied immediately, hoping to reassure her. A consummate hypochondriac, I was typically averse to sharing a choice illness. But this time I wasn't protecting my turf, trying to deter someone from muscling in on my disease. I was actually trying to relieve someone else's anxiety. It was a hugely significant moment for me. I quickly saw that having a real disease could cure my hypochondria.

Once, a doctor stood beside my bed in the hospital and looked over my chart. He told me I'd been dealt a crummy hand. I don't disagree, and I wish the spiritual force behind all this would offer me an explanation. But that's probably not going to happen. It may have been decided somewhere that I need to suffer a bit to learn something important. Still, I picture meeting God face-to-face at the pearly gates one day. I have only one question for him: "What the fuck?!"

I wonder if God sometimes thinks he might have overdone it a little with me. We all make mistakes.

Though it's usually not, MS can be a killer. Thoughts of suicide occasionally wash over me, but so far, I've been hesitant to take that step. I tend to think the road keeps unwinding on the other side, but how can I be sure? Even if the voyage does continue, death may be hiding something worse than anything I've seen. So I'm holding my ground and waiting for the weather to change.

CHAPTER 14

Fall Risk

Liquid Evening

This liquid evening
showers its fragrant bouquet
of wild tendrils reaching for love
across bluing dirt,
like misty skin,
like honey'd blood.
The wind mispronounces its own name,
The vein-crossed leaves
drop like paper bombs
to the waiting ground in ultimate surrender.
Not one angel cries out
not one soul is bruised,
and no stone speaks of regret.

I was sixteen when I got my first guitar. I don't remember why I wanted one—I probably thought it would impress the girls. But I might not have been shooting that high. I could have just wanted to be a rock star. Mine was an unusual entry to that profession. In my early teens, when growing music sensations are learning their instruments and absorbing oceans of musical influences, I played only one radio station. Every night after crawling into bed, I tuned to WPAT, which played primarily soft, cheesy instrumental versions of hit songs from different eras. The music filled long stretches of loaded silences, affording me the peace of mind I needed to fall asleep. I played guitar a lot in those days—very badly—and wrote a lot of terrible songs. My brother and sister would peek in my room occasionally and giggle at my rudimentary attempts to sing and play. That first summer of my independent musical education, I used to escape to the third floor, carrying my guitar out the window, and slide onto the roof to play my songs under the branches of the maple tree. I filled several notebooks with mercifully forgettable lyrics. I found one of those binders recently and flipped through it, shaking my head and grimacing at my expressions of teenage despair:

I'm all alone again,
And no one seems to care.
All my laughter's left
Hanging in the air.

I hoped to sell my songs someday, but I had no idea how to do it. Neither did I care to find out. I wasn't the salesman my father was. He once told me about his interview with IBM, where he sold typewriters for twenty years. His prospective boss reached across the desk and held out a fountain pen. "Roger," he said to my father, "sell me this pen." It's a standard hiring technique, and my father undoubtedly passed with flying colors. But I found any type of selling extremely unpleasant.

To me, back then, poetry was a completely different animal, not a marketable commodity in any degree. And I couldn't see why I'd ever have any contact with it outside the classroom. I still remember needing to recite Wordsworth's poem, *The Daffodils*, in sixth grade. We had a short row of daffodils on the side lawn where I grew up, so the poem appealed to me a little. In general, though, I pretty much managed to avoid having any run-ins with poetry throughout high school. I didn't see the point of reading anything I found so hard to understand and usually seemed to be about nothing important. Most poems sailed past me invisibly and made no impression. When I was a freshman, my English teacher wrote a famous poem on the blackboard:

The Red Wheelbarrow

so much depends
upon

a red wheel
barrow

glazed with rain
water

beside the white
chickens.

Our teacher, a sweet, older woman, told us to copy down the poem, take it home, and write about it, explaining what it was about. I wasn't worried; it seemed like an easy assignment. The poem was short, used simple language, and talked about ordinary, things: a wheelbarrow, rain water, chickens. But when I sat down and read it over, I realized I didn't have the slightest idea what the poem was about. Exactly *what* depended on a red wheelbarrow? So *what* if it was covered with rain and sat beside some chickens? I read it several times and was completely baffled. Finally, I got angry and took my revenge on the poem, pulling out my guitar and turning it into talking blues, rendering it as though I were Bob Dylan.

Years later, when I took English literature in college, I ran across an essay about the poem in my textbook of American verse. But I found the piece as indecipherable as the poem itself. The long-winded literary dissections ran counter to what I had come to like about the poem. I was drawn to its simplicity and felt it was enough to absorb the pictures in the poem, letting them wash over me like a quiet wave.

One July evening, I went to the school's production of *Hamlet*. In the fourth act, Ophelia sings:

How should I your true love know
From another one?
By his cockle hat and staff
And his sandal shoon.

He is dead and gone, lady,
He is dead and gone;

At his head a grass-green turf
At his heels a stone.

I wasn't wild about the music and decided to try my hand at composing something for Ophelia myself. When I got home from the play, I sat down at my father's piano, holding a paperback copy of *Hamlet*. I opened to the lyric I'd just heard Ophelia sing. I read the words out loud a few times and heard a melody in my head. Putting my hands on the keys, I found chords to go with the tune. I would come to believe that melodies are hidden gems buried in the unconscious, like jagged pieces of colored glass. I sang my melody to Shakespeare's words a few times and decided the music fit. A door opened for me. I'd just written my first musical setting. Putting a rocky start behind me, I began reading poems more closely. I would come to love poetry for many reasons: the language and imagery, the rhythms, the intrinsic musicality of many poems. Years later, I would set to music dozens of settings to poems by well-known poets and record four CD's of my musical adaptations of poems by William Blake, Robert Frost, W.B. Yeats, William Shakespeare, and quite a few others.

My favorite collaborator was Emily Dickinson, though I never asked her permission to set her poems. Many of them rested on themes that were very important to me: she wrote about love, god, nature's beauty, and death. The last was not a dark landscape for her. Like Dickinson, I've always seen death as our most important transformation, though I hope not to experience it anytime soon. Many of her verses also use hymn meters, making them ideal for people hoping to use her words as song lyrics. The musical dimensions of Dickinson's writing pulled me in, and I saw that music lengthens a line by slowing down how we take it in. Even if the exact meaning of the poem wasn't clear to me, I felt its emotional tenor from the impression the words made on my ear.

When I finally began thinking about making a CD of my musical settings, I looked around for a studio I might like and could afford. I chose one in a small town a few miles north of me; it was managed by a bright, insightful, musically gifted man named Joe. He was the most accomplished musician I'd ever worked with. He would engineer and play guitar and bass on all five of my CD's. The hours I spent with him in the studio left me feeling deeply indebted to him. I would sit amid instruments and microphone stands and listen to him lay down a guitar or bass track. When I heard Joe create music, I felt inspired, lucky, and grateful. And a little envious.

I always trusted Joe's musical instincts. He had worked with numerous bands over the years, so he was able to recommend a lot of talented musicians. My CD's would include numerous instruments including piano, guitar, cello, bass, drums, flute, organ, oboe, mandolin, and even Scottish bagpipes. One day I asked Joe if he could recommend a percussionist.

"I'm doing a light rock album," he said. "The drummer is a guy named Dan. He's very good, and easy to get along with. I think he's a good bet."

A few days later, I went to the library downtown where Dan served as curator of special collections; two of them included the works of Emily Dickinson and those of Robert Frost. One afternoon I found Dan sitting at his desk in a spacious office on the second floor. The room held a large wooden desk, a sofa, two comfortable chairs, and a fully lined bookcase. I knocked on the open door.

"Can I help you?" he said, looking at me with a smile.

"Hi. Are you Dan?" I asked him.

"Could be," he said. "Unless you're from the IRS. Or the CIA." We both laughed. "How can I help?"

"My name's Sean. I was told you're a great drummer."

"Who paid me such a nice compliment?"

"Joe, the engineer of the album you'll hopefully be playing on. I'm doing an album with him myself, and I'm looking for a percussionist. Are you at all interested?"

"Sure," he said. "I'd love to hear what you do. Can you get me a recording?"

"I'd rather play the song for you," I said.

"Anytime," he said.

"OK, how about this morning around three?"

"Is it a problem if I'm unconscious?" he joked.

I liked him almost immediately and decided that if he were as good as Joe said he was, I would invite him to join the project. I couldn't afford to pay him, or any of the other talented musicians I would work with. Their willingness to pour so much time and energy into the recordings was a tremendous gift.

A few days later, Dan and I met at his place, a small ranch house on a lightly traveled road a few miles from where I lived. I played my setting of the poem, 'Stopping by Woods on a Snowy Evening' for him. Dan said he very much liked what I'd done. Then he led me down the hall to his music room, where he kept his drum set, tambourine, bells, maracas, and bodhran, an Irish hand drum.

I sat on the sofa with my guitar and played the song again while Dan tried different things. First, he took the cymbals off his snares and slid a brush over the top of the drums, creating the soft, dream-like feel of a winter night. In the years to come, Dan would treat me to delightful and fitting percussion parts to my songs. One afternoon while I was visiting him at his second home on Cape Cod, he went downtown for a couple of hours. I got out my guitar and put music to *The Wrong House*, a poem by A. A. Milne. When Dan returned I played it for him.

"Really nice, Sean," he said. When Dan liked something I'd done, I knew I hadn't wasted my time. His approval of my music and the poems I chose to work with meant the world to me.

One day I went to the studio with him. We were going to record my musical rendition of *The Lamentation Of The Old Pensioner*, a poem by W. B. Yeats. I'd long loved the poem, but because of the slowly unwinding transfiguration afoot in my body, *Lamentation* was to become a work I would carry close to my heart.

The Lamentation Of The Old Pensioner

Although I shelter from the rain
Under a broken tree
My chair was nearest to the fire
In every company
That I talked of love or politics,
Ere Time transfigured me.
Though lads are making pikes again
For some conspiracy,
And crazy rascals rage their fill
At human tyranny,

My contemplations are of Time
That has transfigured me.
There's not a woman turns her face
Upon a broken tree,
And yet the beauties that I loved
Are in my memory;
I spit into the face of Time
That has transfigured me.

Being transformed usually means we have undergone some sort of miraculous change, something over which we rejoice. But being *transfigured* normally refers to the unraveling of what was once beautiful, a slow transfiguration of the fabric of our lives. Once I had a dinner date with a woman that didn't go well. I walked across the lobby of the restaurant to greet her; she watched me amble forward slowly carrying my cane. I saw an instantaneous verdict take shape in her eyes. I had become that broken tree, guaranteeing it was over before it started.

A few weeks later, Dan joined my band. We played out a fair amount and were eventually invited to perform at one of the premier music clubs in the area. I had been to this club many times and seen a few of my musical heroes perform there, but I didn't think I'd ever play there myself. The night of the show, we were sitting in the dressing room, where I spent a nervous hour waiting to go on. A scene flashed before my eyes. I saw myself as a teenager, standing under the red spotlight in the cellar of my childhood home strumming my guitar and pretending I was playing to adoring fans.

At some point a woman stuck her head in the door and told us it was time to start. Jeffrey and I would perform first, so we left the room by ourselves and climbed the stairs to the ground floor. In a few moments we were introduced and walked to the stage. As I mounted the steps I noticed with surprise that my nerves had almost completely settled down. Jeffrey and I lifted our guitars off their stands and took our places behind the microphones. I quickly greeted the audience and thanked them for coming. They were wondering what kind of show they would get; I was curious myself. The group of us, seven in all, hadn't rehearsed much. Jeffrey was in well-honed musical form: he played out a lot more than any of us, delivering bluegrass licks on guitar and mandolin for a successful, well-known, local band. I was flattered when I spotted the band's leader in the surprisingly large crowd.

Jeffrey and I launched into our first song, my musical setting of the Frost poem, 'Flower-Gathering,'

I left you in the morning,
And in the morning glow
You walked a way beside me
To make me sad to go...

Our next song was one I had written a few weeks before, a sorrowful look at the end of a romance:

Love, the sadness of your smile
Only seems to grow
Is there something you should say?

Is there something I should know?
Underneath the waves all lovers sail
Lie all the reasons why some love is bound to fail...

    Then Jeffrey and I played my setting of 'Letter to the World,' the title I had given to a poem by Emily Dickinson, who didn't title any of her poems. She seemed to understand the needs of the human heart, and that they were often left unmet. This poem came to weigh heavily on me over the years.

This is my letter to the World
That never wrote to Me –
The simple News that Nature told -
With tender Majesty

Her message is committed
To Hands I cannot see –
For love of Her – Sweet – countrymen –
Judge tenderly – of me.

    I've sent many pleas for healing into the ether but have yet to get a reply. Some of my messages have flirted with despair; that could be why I haven't heard back. Maybe my audience, if I have one, doesn't respond to darkness of any kind.
    Next, my friend, Vernon, brought his cello to the stage and took a chair beside a microphone stand. (Once, I told him we should start a band and call it Vernon Squared.) Tracy, my sister, followed him up. While Vernon was tuning his instrument, I

shared a story with the audience about playing at a nursing home when I was just starting to perform in public. The idea of being on stage for an audience made me very nervous, but I decided playing for seniors was a safe way to begin. I assumed the audience there wouldn't be overly critical. The little crowd of people in front of me was mostly women, and I was pretty sure I probably wouldn't even have their full attention. (I assumed it would be a little like teaching English to college freshman when I was in graduate school in Iowa City.)

As I was finishing my first song, a woman in the front row suddenly spoke up. 'This is *terrible!*" she squawked. "This is *awful.*" It flustered me, and I thought I might not be able to finish the song. But a woman sitting next to her immediately captured my attention. She was wearing a kindly smile, which seemed to say that I shouldn't take the woman's outburst seriously. It immediately soothed me. I played a few more songs, then the activities director walked to the front.

"Are there any questions before we go on?" she asked the group. The woman who had so recently calmed me raised her hand. "Yes, Margaret?" said the activities director.

"Are all the pots and pans for sale?" Margaret asked, looking at the empty space before her.

When I left the building, I saw a resident sitting by herself on a bench next to the driveway. As I went past, I looked at her and smiled.

"Where's your mother buried?!" she blurted at me loudly.

I hurried away and got into my car. It was the first and last time I ever performed in a nursing home. I was ten when I learned about those places. I thought of them as holding cells for death. I was certain I wouldn't choose to spend my last days in one. Ethel Saltus probably felt the same way. Even though she lived in an aging wreck of a once elegant Victorian house, it was *her* wreck.

Unbeknownst to me, one day, a week after I returned, I drove past my old place of employment, thinking I'd stop in on Miss Saltus and make sure she was OK. I hoped a kind person was driving her now and looking after things. But her house was deserted, the bushes sprawling across the driveway. That night, I called her niece, and learned where Miss Saltus had gone. Saddened, I decided to drive over the next day and say hello.

The Florence Nursing Home was a small brick building on a well-manicured lawn. Lilac bushes stood against the front wall, and a green awning hung over the main entrance. One of my chief regrets in life is what I did in the doorway of Miss Saltus' room that day. She was thrilled to see me walk up and immediately asked me take her for a drive. As I looked at her slightly sunken face against the white pillowcase, I was instantly overcome by waves of sorrow. I felt I would drown if I didn't leave immediately; I turned away without a word and walked quickly out the door. I feel badly about that to this day. I hope she forgave me. That would make one of us.

Vernon, Tracy, and I did a song together, with Tracy singing a very sweet harmony. For a moment afterward, I found myself wishing that my older brother and sister were sitting in the audience, so that all four of us were there. I would have found this very gratifying, especially since our parents were permanently elsewhere.

I remember turning around for a moment toward the end of our last set. I smiled briefly at my friend, Larry, who was standing behind me playing bass. Next up was a song I'd named 'Siren.' It talked about a love affair, and referred to the story of Odysseus and the Sirens. Before we began, I gave the audience a short introduction:

"The sirens were mythological creatures who sang so beautifully from the shores of their island, sailors who heard their enchanting song were imprisoned by a powerful spell. It pulled them to the rocky coast where the boat was dashed on the rocks and all the men perished. But Odysseus was determined to avoid this fate. He had his men stop up their ears with wax and had himself lashed to the mast. He wanted to hear, but not fall prey to, the song of the sirens."

Since the onset of my disease, the song had found a new resonance for me. The 'brother' in the song now stood for my body:

Brother of mine, I know where you are
I've heard your small cries of pain
I can't help you now, though I might try,
My intentions are all in vain.

I wasn't thinking of anything so grim while I was singing the song that night. In the years to come, I wouldn't always accord my 'brother' the gentleness and compassion he deserved. In the club that night, I found myself at the highest point I'd ever reached in my very brief musical career. Probably because I thought I might never perform in such a place again, I could hardly bear to leave the club that night. After the show, as the staff began to clean the tables and sweep the floor, I sat on a stool at the bar and took it all in. That's when I got the feeling I was going to take a fall. I didn't know what the universe had in store for me. A fall from grace? A loss of spiritual belief? A fall from a window several stories off the ground? It raised more questions than it answered, but for a few moments, I had a feeling something was coming.

For some time, I had been teaching classes in poetry writing to artistically gifted high school students at a charter school. On my first day, I entered the classroom and sat down at one of the desks. I wanted the students to feel I was one of them. A few minutes after all six students had taken their seats, I smiled at the group and welcomed them. I talked for a bit about how the class would work and told them a little about myself and my experience writing poetry, which was not extensive.

Then I knelt down, opened my guitar case and took out my guitar. I had brought it to class to sing a few of my musical settings of well-known poems. I was confident I would win the admiration of the young poets.

"I'm going to play my setting of *Song For A Dark Girl*," I told them, "a poem by Langston Hughes. He was a Black poet who was part of the Harlem Renaissance. The poem is about the lynching of his lover."

After I finished, no one spoke for several seconds. Then a first-year student raised her hand. I looked at her, eager to get her reaction.

"Can we write now?" she said.

And that's how my career as a high school poetry teacher began. I was to learn a lot about what the students wanted—mostly for their work to be taken seriously by their classmates. As well as by me. They certainly didn't want a teacher who put his own work at a higher level than their own.

My students taught me as much about poetry as I taught them. I always tried to come up with interesting exercises to get their gears turning. Once I took them on a walk down the street to the cemetery. I had them read some epitaphs then compose their own. Another time I had them pair up, look each other in the eye for several seconds, and write a poem about what they saw. They usually looked forward to my assignments, and I always looked forward to their responses.

One evening, I met some of my students at the café in town that held an open poetry reading every Wednesday. I enjoyed hearing them read their poems, and this night was no different. After a couple of hours, I said goodnight to several people and left. As I started to cross the street, I was joined by one of my favorite students, a young man named Jake. He was very popular, especially with the young women. He often made us laugh and wrote brilliant, very dark, poetry.

After leaving the café, Jake and I crossed the street together. When we reached the other side, I raised my foot to clear the curb. But the toe of my shoe struck the curb, and I toppled into the street.

Jake knelt down beside me. "Are you OK?" he asked. He reached out a hand. "Can I help you up?"

"Thanks, but I'm fine," I assured him as I got to my feet.

It was the first time my body had difficulty doing something it had done easily, unconsciously, all of my adult life. It was probably the fall I had sensed was coming in the club that night, a taste of troubles that would begin rolling in. I have been on a slow descent ever since. The trespassing of this disease can apparently not be arrested in me, even though a crime is clearly being committed.

CHAPTER 15

Love Crimes

Angel

She's a different kind of angel;
she doesn't wear wings,
or swoop to catch the dead when they fall.
She speaks to God,
but on her own terms,
in language that feels good on her tongue.
She'll never use deferential tones:
anarchy lets her breathe;
hierarchy never could,
with its stone stairways
and barbed wire gates.
Maps of heaven make her laugh;
no one tells her what circles to patrol,
what thrones are off limits,
or what thoughts she must not think.
She doesn't tread air when the bluebird sings
or blow a silver trumpet when Gabriel calls.

But she will move to your side when sorrow comes,
and she will turn a soft ear
when your heart is bound by a trail of stars
that have tumbled from the sky.
Happiness is a prize she guards without apology
or the blush of guilt.
She won't lay herself down like a pool
to catch other's tears,
won't deal in counterfeits for people to admire.
She will leave you to your own dominions,
but she will stand on the border
between your calling and hers,
and you will feel her there.

I'm not going to give you a blow-by-blow account of the years I spent as Lesley's partner. That would be a love story, and that's not what this is. Not exactly. It took a while for the story Lesley and I were composing to reach any sort of conclusion. Getting to what feels like a finish line in the often rugged terrain of the heart requires a commitment to follow a trail to the end. But I don't want to finish telling the story before I lay myself down and take a breath.

Often, you know exactly what the other person wants before the two of you even leave the starting gate. With Lesley, I didn't know right away. I'm still not sure what she wanted, and she never gave me much help on this. I don't think she knew, either.

Even though my faith in us constantly wavered, I managed to believe everything was fine, that our relationship might last a lifetime. I sometimes think that if my parents had remained together I might actually believe in happy endings, even for myself. Still, I often wondered why anyone would consider me a feasible lifetime partner given my shaky health. To me, there was no question my physical challenges would always be an issue for Lesley and me. Given the landscape she wanted in her life, she really couldn't stay with me. She'd have to give up too many things, like walking in the woods with her partner, or taking a turn in the passenger seat on long drives.

I came into contact with Lesley on an online dating site, a place where people share personal information up front, to avoid wasting time. In her profile, Lesley said she had been married, raised two kids, earned a B.A. in anthropology, and had received a graduate degree in education. She'd taught ESL, and published three books. She said her partner would need a lot of energy to keep up with her.

She wrote first.

Hi Sean,

I like your profile. I'm a writer, living in the Berkshires. I'm a teacher too. Seems we have a lot in common. What do you think?

~Lesley

I thought about what I would say when I replied, or what I *wouldn't* say. I could tell her about my own family, my education, and all the rest of it, but what would I say about my health? Giving her the full story right off the bat would ensure that no time was wasted, and yet I hesitated, an effective technique for wasting it. I went to sleep that night in full-throttle hesitation. To me, Lesley was smart, talented, attractive, and funny, and I quickly decided I wouldn't write her back.

But she wrote me again the next day.

Sean,

It would be nice to talk with someone who understands what it's like to be a writer. Also, I forgot to say that I'm very sorry about your cat. I had that kind of love with a Siamese once and I still miss her after all these years.

I hope you write back.

~Lesley

That got me. If the right woman touched one of my soft spots, she would undoubtedly get my attention. I was positive I'd be taking a long shot now when it came to love and couldn't expect anything more. I decided to take a chance.

Lesley,

So here I am replying. Thanks for your kind words about the cat I lost several months ago. I still have the box with her ashes on my dresser.

Where are you from? If you're from someplace other than western Massachusetts, how did you end up here?
~Sean

Hi Sean,

You're most welcome. I can really relate. My cat died in my arms several years ago. Her picture is still at my bedside.

I'm from the suburbs, just outside of New York City. I've been here for many years now, so I consider myself a local, no longer a New Yorker. I lost my job when Reagan slashed the non-profit budgets, so I moved up here to get away from the city. Now I'm a writer and teacher.

What about you? Are you from somewhere else?
~Lesley

Lesley,

I'm from New Jersey. I taught English in a charter high school up here for 10 years. Then I got sick, with a condition I deal with every day. I'll tell you more about it if I get to know you better and feel confident you won't run for the hills.
~Sean

Sean,

On your profile page you said you were looking to make new friends. You didn't say anything about long term, so I'm hoping your illness will not prevent this possibility for you. I am not running for the hills. Unless you're a leper. Are you a leper? I might run if your nose has fallen off. I'd like to make you one of my new friends. And who knows? You might run after reading some of my books. I liked your profile picture.
~Lesley

Hi.

Thanks for not running, though, to be fair, you don't know what you're dealing with. No, it's not leprosy. Nothing has fallen off my body. It's MS, a mysterious illness. I first saw symptoms when I was 28. The neurologist I consulted said the seizure and the numbness in my arm could be early signs of MS, but probably not. After being diagnosed, I decided to go the alternative route and followed it for a few years. It included acupuncture, chiropractic, cranio-sacral, dietary changes, and many other things. When none of that stopped the progression or turned it around, I decided to try a more conventional route. I went twice to an MS clinic in Manhattan, where a doctor administered a drug via a spinal tap.

There are other lovely things I could tell you, but that's enough for right now. Maybe forever. It could well seal the deal. Or unseal any deal we might make. I have no shortage of things to choose from, but the 'driving piece' weighs heavily on my mind. I'm thinking that you live on the western edge of the state, over an hour's drive away.

Despite all this, I still think I might find a woman who's OK with having a partner who's far from physically perfect. I know it's not my fault, and that, like anyone, I deserve compassion. But I struggle with forgiving myself.

~Sean

Hi. Thanks a lot for sharing that. And, guess what, I'm still here. I do know about MS, though not directly. I knew someone who had it, so I know it's not fun. I'm so sad that you can no longer do many things you loved. But you can still walk and play guitar… I'm sorry you can't drive anymore. But I do drive, and I come frequently to your neck of the woods. And I know there are plenty of coffee shops there. Would you care to have a cup with me? And who knows? Maybe your new treatment will work. I truly believe in a higher power, and

I think the most important thing you can do is to love and forgive yourself and do what brings you joy. I believe that the more we focus on the positive, the more it appears. I was thinking about Marianne Williamson's famous quote: "It is our light, not our darkness, that most frightens us."
~Lesley,

Lesley,

Thank you for being so compassionate. I love the quote. It seems to speak to both of us. Yes, let's meet for coffee. Tomorrow too soon?
~Sean

Hi.

Then I will have to watch, 'Jane Eyre' this evening. I must get a whopping dose of romance before tomorrow.

Nervous. Excited.

~Lesley

At one time in her life, Lesley had a partner with Chronic Fatigue Syndrome, which left him too weak to do a lot of the things Lesley wanted to do with a partner. That incapacity had become the crux of my insecurity. I wondered if she would want me as a partner. In the days when I was healthy, I don't know that I would have chosen to be with a handicapped woman. So how could I fault anyone for feeling the same? I once heard a woman respond to a friend who asked her if she'd ever get involved with a handicapped man: "It would depend on the handicap," the woman replied. She explained to her friend that if it was jealous rage or some other disturbing, possibly dangerous thing, she would stay far away. Then she said that if the person had physical problems because of an accident or illness, she didn't see why not. I considered it a noble thing to say, but I didn't believe her for a second. Because of one partner, Lesley had already spent time on the road I travel. I figured she might accompany me for a while but that in the end, she would look for an easier way. I wouldn't blame her.

We met at a little Italian café down the street from my apartment. I got there first. I was using my cane and walking beside Donna, my PCA, who was carrying a few of the CDs I had made over the years, as well as a bouquet of spring flowers I'd bought for the occasion. I chose a table against the windows and sat down, resting my cane against the edge of the table. I had almost bought roses, but decided giving them to her might seem a little forward and presumptuous. Having seen a picture of her on the website, I was sure I'd recognize her and sat back to wait. Donna wished me luck and left the café.

I was glad to be sitting down; Lesley wouldn't see that my gait was unsteady. It was the most visible in a list of physical impediments that the universe had generously donated to me. The collection of symptoms had been slowly blossoming for years, but I wasn't anxious for Lesley to know that. I worried it might take me out of the running before we even started. When we'd talked on the phone, she told me she thought MS was a death sentence and didn't need long to finish the job. I informed her that despite its many colorful trappings, the disease would probably allow me to live a life of nearly normal length. That would be enough for any couple to deal with, and there were a number of unattractive details about living with the condition. I didn't want to share this. Not yet.

Sitting alone at the table, I started to worry. What if she was a terrible writer? Would I have to lie to avoid hurting her feelings? But I was getting ahead of myself. I resolved to turn off my mind and just wait. A few minutes later, a woman entered the café. She stood a little over 5 feet tall, wasn't skinny or heavy, and was pretty with a creamy complexion. She was wearing blue jeans and an attractive, turquoise shirt. She walked right over to my table and looked at me through pretty blue-green eyes.

"I'm thinking you must be Sean," she said.

"I'm thinking you are right!" I replied. "These are for you." I handed her the flowers.

"Thank you," she said. "They're lovely.

We shook hands and she pulled out the chair across from mine and sat down.

"These are also for you," I said, sliding my CDs across the table. "It's okay if you hate them."

"I doubt I'll hate them," she laughed. Then she slid a few books my way. "Read these if you want," she said. "I hope you like them."

At first, I thought reading her books was optional for me, just as she thought listening to my music was optional for *her*.

But in both cases it wasn't. Not if we wanted to go forward, dive beneath the surface, and explore. We each very much wanted to impress the other, so we put what we believed was our best foot forward and took a step.

I was quiet for a moment. "So, I take it you've been to this town before," I said.

"Absolutely," she answered. "Lots of times. My daughter and I love to shop for clothes here. They have some great stores on this street."

"That's why I moved here," I said smiling.

For a half hour we traded details of our lives. "I guess we need to ask each other for our favorite writers, now," I said. "This could very well decide things."

"OK, pressure," she said, her eyes twinkling. "For me, it's easy. Charlotte Bronte. I read 'Jane Eyre' every year. It's kind of a ritual with me. How about you? Who's your favorite poet?"

"Emily Dickinson," I answered quickly. 'She said this world is not conclusion.' I hope she's right about that. Most days I'm pretty sure she is."

"I *know* she is," Lesley said.

I decided not to tell her that I'd probably grown up in a haunted house. For me, that was a serious subject, and I was trying to keep things light. I couldn't think of anyone I enjoyed talking to more. I was hoping she felt the same way, or something close. I found it easy to talk to her, and I wasn't afraid we'd run out of things to say anytime soon. I asked her if she wanted to see my apartment before going home.

"I'd love to," she said. "How do we get there?"

"Follow me," I said, getting out of my chair, standing up and steadying myself. "It's only two blocks away."

We left the café together and turned down the sidewalk.

Several minutes later we came to my building. I was relieved there was no one around—no drug dealers, no monks, nobody at all. It was peaceful, and in that building, peace was not typically the order of the day. We took the elevator to the fifth floor, got out, and walked down the hall to my apartment. Inside, I introduced her to my black and gold cat, Zanzibar, who looked her over and automatically started rubbing against her ankle. I asked Lesley if she wanted a snack. She thanked me and politely declined. Then she knelt and ran a hand down Zanzibar's back. I sat down on the couch and asked her if she wanted to join me. The question was bigger than it sounded, and I was bound to think her answer highly significant. She sat down next to me, and we went on talking for a while. Then I leaned over, and we kissed.

An hour later, we rode the elevator together to the ground floor. Then we crossed the lobby and stopped.

"That was fun," she said, smiling at me. "I'm glad I came over."

"We're going to see each other again, aren't we?" I asked. I said it with a smile, but I was a little nervous. "I mean, after you drive off, we might both feel relieved it's over."

"Well, it *is* a very long drive, and gas isn't cheap. "

"Yes, but you won't find better clothes anywhere."

"Well, that's true," she said. "And these cafes have really good coffee."

We both laughed a little and looked at each other. Then I leaned over and we kissed each other goodbye. She pushed open the door and left. I knew another door had just opened. As Lesley walked away, she turned to me and waved. I waved back.

Our journey had barely begun, and though we had no idea where it would take us, we each wanted very much to be on it. I wasn't yet able to articulate it, but deep down, I knew that if Lesley hadn't been breathing the same air I breathe, I might feel a little lonely. That's usually not terribly significant, but loneliness is an atmosphere I've had a little too much of in my life. In time, I would find the fresh oxygen Lesley blew into my lungs could be charged in all kinds of ways, both good and bad. But after getting my first lungful of it, I had no doubt I was alive.

Lesley lived in a house on the western edge of the state. If I still drove, the distance wouldn't have mattered. But the disease has made issues of things that had never caused problems before. I realize now that I probably might never drive again; if Lesley and I had lived closer together, we might have had a better chance of success as a couple. But even then there would still be mountains to scale and put behind us.

Lesley and I started to spend a lot of our days and nights together, mostly in her four bedroom house on an acre of land at the foothills of the Berkshires in western Massachusetts. We did a lot of things the average couple does, but I often needed more than an average amount of help. Lesley would assist me with things that came effortlessly to most people: she held onto me when I climbed over the tub wall, got me on and off the toilet, and took my arm when I climbed the stairs. But we talked endlessly, sometimes made each other laugh so hard we shook, wrote songs together, walked arm and arm through town, sat on a beach and strolled to the water.

I don't know what arms I could have taken against the sea of troubles I'd dropped into because of my feelings for Lesley. I wanted to believe that she and I would be together forever, and not just as friends. I know that life can rush by, and so can people. I had already started to worry that Lesley might soon be one of them. Even before my disease entered the picture, I gave worry a little too much play. My therapist, Judy, once told me that Lesley's arrival in my life marked the first time I had been in love. I asked Judy why she'd said that. "It's because she's the first person whose happiness is as important to you as your own."

Lesley was the only girlfriend of mine who made me feel I wasn't the most important person in her life. I would realize that the first time I saw them together. It was instantly clear to me that her kids, who were in their late teens, had profoundly captured their mother's heart. I needed time to get used to the order I'd fallen into, and it would prove to be a fairly steep rise. Lesley was my first partner whose life included children, real ones, not adults who hadn't completely grown up yet. At first, I would think Lesley a better parent than my own. In some ways, she probably was, but I had yet to understand that a person can love in secret. My parents loved me, but sometimes it was hard to see.

When I fell in love with Lesley, I had climbed onto a slippery ladder. I stood on a rung closer to the top than where I would be a few years later. During our early days together, Lesley took me to quite a number of medical clinics and alternative healers of every stripe. I tried anything that promised results. I read about a man who so desperately wanted to be well he traveled thousands of miles to the Amazon jungle to see an indigenous healer.

We even flew to Miami, Florida so that I could receive an infusion of stem cells. I lay on a padded table and received them intravenously into my arm. The needle was withdrawn after a couple hours, and I started waiting for something to happen. The second day, Lesley and I swam in the crystal blue ocean and laughed together as we rode the waves, feeling that we were on the edge of a world where the future was no longer something to fear.

"Can we see Cuba from here?" I asked her, ocean water rising over my chest.

"I'm not sure," Lesley replied, looking at the horizon. "Let's just imagine that we can."

I pointed ahead. "That could be Cuba, right there."

Lesley looked at the strip of land. "Do you suppose someone is standing over there pointing toward us asking if this could be Florida?'

"Don't know," I said. "Possibly. Do you think they're jealous?"

"Hard to say. Maybe grateful."

I thought for a minute. "That's how I feel with you," I said. Lesley reached up and lay her arms on my shoulders.

The day we returned after our first visit to Miami, I walked through Lesley's kitchen without a cane, stretching my arms out to either side displaying perfect balance. That morning, I sat on the toilet and emptied my bladder without using the dreaded catheter. To me, that was nothing short of miraculous. But, after a week, those extremely hopeful signs disappeared. Soon, I was right back to where I had been, muscles all over my body failing to cooperate. Two years later, Lesley and I returned to Miami, hoping a second injection of stem cells might do the trick. On our first morning there, we went downstairs to the pool behind the hotel. Lesley trotted off by herself to swim in the ocean, while I stayed behind in the hotel swimming pool. I felt much weaker than I had the year before. I sensed a rung on the ladder give way. We didn't admit it, even to ourselves, but we'd lost hope that stem cells might stop the train I was on.

A month later, we started looking into the medicinal

powers of peyote. We decided to hold a peyote ceremony in Lesley's back yard. We learned that peyote contains mescaline, a hallucinogen from a small cactus that lives in parts of Mexico and southwestern Texas. I read that ingesting peyote can give a person profound insights their psychological and spiritual dimensions. We read that peyote has cured people of irreversible disease, sometimes pulling them out of their wheelchairs. I was now forced to use a wheelchair when I needed to go uphill or travel more than a few blocks. I hadn't become completely dependent on the chair yet, but I could feel myself heading in that direction. I was very excited about using the peyote and not at all afraid.

One Friday afternoon toward the end May, about twenty people drove to Lesley's house from all over New England and beyond. Four Navajos drove in from Arizona. Several men hammered metal stakes into lawn behind Lesley's house and raised a twenty-five foot tall, white canvas teepee. That night, we all sit inside it on the edge of a large fire inside a ring of large stones.

At the start of the ceremony, individuals spoke about anything they thought important to share, most of them wishing me well on my quest to recapture my physical health and receive any important messages. After a couple of hours, two friends helped me stand and helped me walk around the fire circle. I quickly saw it was going to be a difficult trip, and within seconds I thought I'd made a very bad mistake. But my friends eventually got me back to my seat and helped me as I collapsed into it.

For the next several hours, people played water drums and sang songs of the Ojibwe and Navajo people and those of other tribes. Two medicine men prayed over me during the course of the night and chanted in languages I didn't understand. I chewed several handfuls of peyote buttons, drank a couple cups of peyote tea, and smoked tobacco through rolled corn leaves. Lesley sat on one side of me, a friend of mine sat on the other. The peyote, a stimulant, kept us wide awake all night. It was possibly the most hopeful, exhilarating night of my life. I don't remember ever feeling so happy. In the morning, I stepped out of the tepee and stood in Lesley's back yard, where I'd been many times. For half a minute I had no idea where I was. It's exactly what one of the medicine men told me would happen.

For a few weeks after the ceremony, my happiness was unshakable, and I had surprising insights into my thinking and beliefs. I thought my body was on the brink of transformation, a return to life under sunny skies, where no dark shapes lurked around the next bend. I was hoping for a miraculous deliverance, a total resetting of the clocks in my body. The words, "Magic is happening," materialized in my mind one early morning, while riding home in my wheelchair after a swim at the YMCA. The message, "Your body is working very hard," came into my head one night as I was falling asleep. Every cell in my brain opened to the hope that profound healing *was* underway in the cells of my body. But after weeks of waiting for a clear sign of physical change, I had to accept that no miracle was unfolding. After years of making every effort to turn things around on the physical plane, I felt myself plunging past the lowest rung on the ladder. I was out of ideas for how I might arrive at a halt to my downward slide, or even a reversal. I had lost what little hope I had left. I think Lesley had too. And the night I fell down hard on the stone pathway leading to her house might well have been the breaking point.

A week later, Lesley called me. She asked me a question that worried me a little. "Can I come to your therapy tomorrow?"

"I guess so," I answered. "What do you want to talk about? That's kind of a sacred hour for me."

"I know it is," she said, "and I don't wanted to steal it from you. But I need to talk about our relationship."

Suddenly I had a fluttering in my gut. I tried not to think the worst, though, for that has become my standard response when I sense trouble.

"OK, if it's really important to you, let's sit down with her," I said. I told myself I was doing the right thing, and I tried hard to believe it. I thought it best to be optimistic, especially in a troubling situation.

Judy's office was in the center of town, a half mile from my apartment. On the phone, Lesley told me she would be very busy that morning and would get to my town with just a few minutes to spare. We decided to meet outside Judy's building and go straight up to her office. When it came time to leave my apartment that morning, I climbed into my wheelchair and set off. I found Lesley waiting for me at the bottom of the ramp into Judy's building. As it turned out, my worst fear awaited me there that day.

"I don't think I can be Sean's girlfriend anymore," Lesley announced quietly that morning in Judy's office. "I'm in love with him, and he's my best friend, but I need our relationship to change. I really think we'll be much better as friends."

Judy looked at me. I gathered myself for a moment and thought about what to say. I wanted to sound like I wasn't surprised or the least bit upset. "We haven't been happy with things for a long time," I said, forcing a smile. "This had to happen. And I'm fine with it. Things are going to be much better in our relationship. Whatever it is now." Judy looked at me skeptically. She knew I wasn't at all sure about that. I don't think Lesley was, either.

"Have you wanted to say that for a long time?" Judy asked Lesley.

"Pretty long," she returned, looking down. I saw a tear fall. We went silent again.

"Sean, what are you feeling?" Judy looked at me directly.

"This is pretty hard to hear."

"You both deserve admiration for having this talk. I know this has been hard for both of you. Lesley, having a partner with such a debilitating disease can't be easy."

Lesley nodded, not looking at either of us.

"And Sean, you have had love for the first time in your life, and Lesley still loves you, but for her, things need to be different. Can you respect that?"

"I understand, but I wish things could have turned out differently." And then I began to cry. Lesley was already crying.

"This is heartbreaking," Lesley said. "I'm so sorry."

We cried for some time. Judy handed us tissues. After the 50 minutes were up, we stumbled out of the office.

"Do you want to get a cup of tea?" I asked.

"OK," she answered. "Where should we go?"

"How about that cafe at the end of the street?" I said, pointing to it.

"Sure," she answered. "I like that place."

It would take us several minutes to get there. I maneuvered my chair down the street while Lesley walked slowly to stay even with me. In the café, I rolled over to a table while Lesley went to the counter and ordered two cups of peppermint tea. We sat at our table quietly, glancing at the people around us. When we talked, it felt a little forced. A young woman quickly brought us a pot of tea and set the pitcher and cups on the table. I couldn't remember Lesley and I ever having so little to say to each other. We sipped the tea in near silence for a few minutes.

"Let's get out of here," she said, after we finished our tea.

"Yeah, let's," I said. We headed to the door.

"You do know I'll never leave you," Lesley said, grasping my elbow as we stood at the curb.

"Of course," I said, knowing it was what she wanted to hear. The truth was, I felt she was already on her way. I couldn't blame her. We'd had such high hopes for the life we were going to have together. That life seemed permanently out of reach now.

Lesley had loved me, and no doubt she still did, though in a heartbreakingly diminished way. Because of her, I own a long list of priceless memories. I remember lying beside her on the beach, laughing as hard as I ever have, and after a minute laughing again. I see us lounging on her couch writing songs together. Once, we floated in the ocean, holding each other and feeling the current pushing against our legs. I remember playing with her dogs in the waving grass. On our way to sleep, we would lie close to each other under the blankets and hold hands, the stars winking and somehow helping me see that all I really have to do is learn to enjoy some of the sweetest moments I will ever know. I would feel so blessed if I could once again blend into a crowd and disappear. I want to climb off the stage my disease dragged me onto without my consent. I long to walk up that aisle by myself, leave the theater through the front door, and step into the nameless crowd. I would search for her face. I'd find her there, looking back at me.

The First Time

The first time I held you
was the first time I never wanted to let something go.
In that moment a seed of wonder was born;
one watered daily by your animal grace,
your measureless faith in the goodness brimming
in even the most washed out version of the human soul.
One night I watched you sleep;
I could weep hot tears
to think of the silvery light of that April moon,
sparkling like a spring pool across your cheek—
for my happiness ensures that I have joyful tears enough
and a way to keep them warm.

CHAPTER 16

Surfacing

Vow

Before whatever is going to happen to me has happened,
I will throw open the shutters
and let the rain blow in,
I will watch Nature's mysterious potions
infiltrate my blossoming soul.
While I am still deep in the life-bed tangle,
inundated with desire,
regretting nothing I have done
or left undone,
I resolve to love
not sporadically,
never half-heartedly,
not in crystal fragments,
but with a drenching pulse,
like a flood tide over-spilling its banks.
In the winking of a star,
my weary body will sink down

into the arms of the primordial mother
and vaguely decay,
becoming one with the earth.
But before that happens
and the blue horizon slips out of sight,
I will glide through layers of memory,
feeling reverberations of spring-times past
sweeping over me
like a fragrant, forgotten breeze,
fever pushing up through leaf mold
to rinse itself in light.
Before any of that happens,
I will love this world without exception
or dark vibration,
I will love it all now,
as long as now shall last.

One night around 9:30, I was sitting at my dining room table and decided to turn in. After making my nighttime trip to the bathroom, I rolled out and parked next to my bed. When I got out of my chair and went to stand up I suddenly lost my balance and toppled, slamming my right side into the linoleum floor. After trying several times to get up, I reached up and pulled the phone off my nightstand. I dialed Dan's number and told him I had fallen and was lying on the floor. I asked if he could possibly drive over and help me into bed. Ten minutes later, Dan opened the door to my apartment. He used the key I had given him in case I should ever be in this very situation. A year later, finding my memory a little shaky on the event, I wrote to Dan and asked what he remembered.

Sean,

I remember the night you called and I drove to your place and found you waiting patiently on the floor. I helped you back onto the bed. We talked a bit, then you asked for help into the bathroom. I watched from outside the door to make sure you were alright then helped you into the bed again. I remember it was a bit difficult to help you slide up so your head rested comfortably on the pillow. I especially recall how tender I felt toward you. How it was an honor to be trusted enough to share the intimacy of a time when you needed someone to help you do something as simple as getting back into bed. It was humbling.

~ Dan

Humbling? I wondered if Dan placed me on higher ground somehow. Did he think he wouldn't be able to live a life like mine, with its physical and emotional losses and challenges? After he got me back into the bed that night, Dan asked me what had happened.

"I fell," I told him.

"I can see that," he laughed. "Why did you fall?"

"I don't know. I'm not always sure why I fall. Maybe I have an infection. Maybe I'm just tired."

Dan was quiet for a moment. "MS makes you weak, doesn't it?" he said. Dan seemed careful not to ask me certain questions. He may have been afraid of trespassing on private territory. But I've never had secrets from people close to me. "The right side of my body is weaker than the left. It's hard for me to lift my right foot very high off the ground, for instance. And I can't really write longhand anymore."

"Yes, but you can still play guitar," said Dan. "That's great!"

"Yeah, I can still play the guitar, but not like I used to. My arms don't move smoothly anymore. I don't feel sorry for myself, but I've never been very good at saying goodbye to things that are important to me. And some things are harder to part with than others."

The next morning, I decided to get an x-ray to make sure I hadn't broken anything. I went to the hospital in a van for the handicapped. As an intern pushed me down the hospital corridors to radiology, I found myself wondering how many hours I've spent at hospitals in my life. I'm curious to know, but not all that much. I want to be as happy as I can, so I always try to stay off dead end streets. No doubt, a few of those visits have saved my life, and I'm not sufficiently grateful. I often strike out in that department. None of the multitude of things I've done to restore my health has gotten the job done, or even stopped the slide.

After they took pictures of my leg, I was guided back to the radiology waiting area. In a little while, a doctor's assistant walked up and sat down on the sofa beside me. She told me they'd read the report about my accident and that they assumed it was caused by weakness in my legs, due to the MS, an infection, or both. She advised me to have a blood test at the hospital that night and check into a rehabilitation facility tomorrow. The following day, I entered a nearby clinic. I didn't know I had spent my last day in MacDougall. My train was pulling out of that station.

For two days I did simple exercises on the mat and the cushioned table. I had considerable pain in my right leg. I told my physical therapist about it, and she didn't seem to think anything of it. But the next morning, I woke up knowing something was wrong with my leg. I decided I wanted more x-rays. I knew a fresh break often doesn't show up in the pictures. A minute after I pulled the cord, one of the aides stopped in. I told her I wanted another x-ray of my leg. That day if possible. She told me she would have a nurse come talk to me and left the room. Soon the nurse came in. I informed her what I'd told the aide, and she said they would call an ambulance and have it take me back to the hospital where this had all started. She helped me clean up and get dressed and transfer to my wheelchair. There I waited for the van to arrive.

Suddenly, I wanted to hear Lesley's voice. Not much had really changed since that day in Judy's office. We had definitely broken up, but we still phoned each other almost every day. And we still saw each other regularly. Lesley would drive out to my town and spend the day with me. Given the slow worsening of my condition, we couldn't do all that much anymore. But we still toured the downtown area, went out for meals, drove through the countryside, sat outside and listened to the birds. And we still held each other, even if we didn't touch as we once did. I really didn't have that much reason to complain, especially since I could be in far worse shape.

She had been in Italy for a few days with her parents and both sisters. I didn't know exactly where she was, but she usually had her cell phone nearby. I had grown used to Lesley being there for me, and this day I really needed her. I didn't know the fine details of her life anymore; I tried to persuade myself I didn't care. But I did care. I cared more than I wanted to. It hampered my ability to focus on things I could control.

As her phone rang, I thought I was doing something I would probably regret. I was sure she'd had enough of coming to my rescue. If she was feeling that way, I wouldn't have blamed her. I've often wondered if my illness formed the ground of our being together. Did I need someone I could count on to rescue me? I'd long thought I might be the remedy to her feeling she hadn't always mattered enough to people she truly cared about.

"Hello," she said, on picking up the phone.

"Hi," I said. "Is this a bad time?"

"No, it's fine. Guess where I am."

"I don't know," I said. "The Great Wall of China?"

"I'm in Venice," she told me.

"Are you floating on one of those canals in a granola?"

"Gondola."

"I was kidding. At least I think I was kidding. Isn't it great I still have a sense of humor?"

"Yeah, such as it is."

"You know, Italy isn't that far away," I reminded her. "When did you get to Venice, anyway?"

"I flew into the country by myself a couple of days ago. Then I drove here and met up with everybody."

"Boy, I might be a little envious if I weren't in Italy, myself! I'm here in Rome."

"Rome?" she said, feigning amazement. "That's awesome!"

"Yeah! I ran into Gregory Peck and Audrey Hepburn yesterday. I think they're making a movie. Sad to say, I almost never speak with either of them anymore."

"I don't think you really need the 'anymore,'" Lesley laughed. It was a sound I'd have missed if I didn't hear it anymore. I was glad she was still in my life, although it was different. We hadn't spoken since she left for Italy and I'm glad she answered.

"This is boring compared to what you're doing," I said. "but I'm actually sitting on my bed in a rehab clinic. This is my third day."

"What?!" she said, sounding a little alarmed. "What happened? Are you all right?!"

"Yeah, I'm fine. I fell on my bedroom floor. The problem is, I think I might have injured my leg. I've already had an x-ray, and they said there was nothing wrong. I know I'm a hypochondriac but I just don't believe nothing's wrong."

"I've heard that fresh breaks don't always show in x-rays right away," Lesley said. "Maybe this is one of those cases. I sure hope not."

My break with Lesley showed up right away and it hurt. I knew from experience that heartbreak can lay in hiding a long time. But I felt the fallout from losing Lesley the moment it happened.

"Maybe you should get more pictures," she said.

"I know. I'm having some more taken tomorrow."

"Great! That's very smart. Look, I have to get back to my parents, but let's please talk tomorrow." I promised her I'd call.

I got another set of x-rays that morning. After the technicians finished taking their pictures, I was wheeled to the lobby. I'd been told someone would talk to me about what the x-rays showed. Eventually, an intern walked up and explained that the x-ray showed a long break in my femur, the thigh bone that connects to the hip. I was not surprised, but I was upset that I had been using a broken leg and may have further damaged it.

He said they wanted to do surgery that night. They would put a pin in my leg to secure the femur.

I was moved to a room upstairs. A few hours later, while I was lying on my bed, a nurse stopped in. She told me I would be brought downstairs for surgery in a few hours. After she left the room, I called Lesley to give her an update.

"Hi," I said. "I've got some late-breaking news. Want to hear it?"

"Of course I want to hear it! What did the x-ray show?"

"My femur's broken," I said. "They're going to fix me up around midnight."

"Why so late?"

"I guess they don't want to wait until tomorrow."

"You just don't get a goddamn break!" She said. "You must have been an awful person in a past life."

"Maybe. How do you think I'm doing in this one?" I laughed. "Maybe my sins haven't been forgiven yet upstairs."

"Maybe there's more to learn," Lesley said.

Lesley cleared her throat. When she went on, she was a little choked up.

"You do know I love you, right?" she said. "I was sobbing for a while after we talked." For Lesley, love was an important word, but she had a very hard time getting it out. "I know it's been a rough ride for you," she said. "You know I've been there for a lot of it. It's been hard on me, too. Sometimes I'm really angry with you. But I realize it's not you, it's this horrible disease. It's made the life I wanted impossible. The life with you."

"I've lost a lot, too," I said, knowing I didn't need to say it. Lesley had done more for me than anyone else. Infinitely more.

"Please call me tomorrow and tell me how it went. Do that for me, alright?"

"Of course, I will." It meant the world to me that she asked.

A few days after my surgery, I was sent to a rehab clinic nearly an hour away from my home and my sister, and two hours away from Lesley. I was completely alone. When she returned from Italy, she went into high gear to help me get out of that clinic. First, she found a small rehab hospital in the Berkshires with an empty bed, just five miles from her home. I was moved there the next day. The head of the unit's physical therapy department told me healing from injuries like mine would take a healthy person several weeks. He said that for me, it would likely take a few months. I moved into a single room at the end of the hall on the main floor, and got into a very workable daily routine. I had physical therapy twice every day, taking three walks up and down the hall in each session. I ate hospital-quality food, which meant the food was edible and not much more. I didn't sleep well there, and almost every night I rode the elevator down to the basement. It contained a few offices, a meeting room, and a small gym. I pushed myself up and down the linoleum floor in perfect silence; most nights, an orange cat kept me company on my solitary journey.

There was an isolated bedroom on one of the corridors. I always passed the room cautiously: through the pane of glass in the door, I could see the room's only bed. The mound of the sleeper's body lay under the blankets. I never saw the person ever move or breathe, and no nurse ever looked in to make sure the tenant was alive. Toward the end of my second month in the facility, I got brave one night and decided to stick my head in the room and have a look. I slowly opened the door and wheeled into the room a foot at a time, heading for the bed. I listened very closely as I approached, straining my ears for the slightest sound. I reached the curtain a foot away from the bed and stopped. In a moment I burst with laughter. The bed's only occupant was a life-size Styrofoam dummy. I turned my chair around, and standing at the door was the orange cat, who seemed to be looking at me with amusement. There must be times when an animal is grateful not to be human.

Eventually, the day came for me to visit my vacant apartment and see if I was ready, and able, to go home. In the morning, Jenny, a PT at the clinic, drove me to the building where I'd been living for almost ten years. In about an hour, we were driving through the center of my town, along streets I used to creep down in my wheelchair every day. I took in sights I worried I'd never see again. It felt good to be back.

I only had a few friends left in those parts. Some had moved away from the area, others just from me. A friend who had a chronic condition that prevented her from going too far from home told me she'd lost a lot of friends because of it. When my illness cast its net over me, friends began drifting into the shadows. But the town still felt like home, and it seemed to welcome me back. When I went into my apartment, I felt nothing had changed. The sun was filtering through the trees beyond the parking lot, and I just wanted to climb into the comfortable chair on the deck and take a breath. But my days climbing into chairs easily and safely were gone. Suddenly, I started to remember what my life there had been like at the end. I fell more often, at least once a month, and I often lay on the floor by myself in my bedroom or the bathroom for up to an hour. There was a cord on the wall to call for help, but I was usually unable to reach it. I never even asked any of the staff if the building was equipped with alarms. I was no longer sure I wanted to return to the remnants of my old life.

By the time I got back to my new, temporary home down the road from Lesley, I had pretty much decided that what I thought of as home fell far short of that word. Lesley was still my best friend, as she'd been since we'd fallen in love. Every day, she stopped in to see me at the rehab center. Sometimes she would guide my wheelchair up the sidewalk to a popular Indian restaurant. Other times we'd sit on the front porch, just down from my room. We'd talk about today, and yesterday, but never about tomorrow. Neither of us had a solid idea what our future together looked like. We didn't really know what we were to each other now, besides terribly important. And we didn't want to overstep the slippery definition.

One day, Lesley and I shared a ride in a most uncomfortable van that took us an hour and a half from the rehab facility to the university medical center. I had an appointment with a neurologist at the university hospital's MS clinic. The doctor showed me the latest MRI of my brain, pictures I had never seen, only because I didn't want to see them. Lesley sat beside me on the couch as we looked at graphic, crystal-clear pictures of the terrain very much in question. I couldn't look at the images without fighting back tears, the runway of my steadily dwindling hope.

It might not have been until I sat there, looking at pictures of my battered grey matter, that everything came into focus for me. I finally accepted, without hope of a magical healing, that my disease would probably keep tearing at the sinews of my body as long as it could. As my brother used to say of his own inevitable demise, he would be around until there was nothing left for death to take. That line usually raised uncomfortable laughter in me, but I never stepped fully out of the shadow of those words. My brother was a very funny man, and dark humor was part of his repertoire.

After we returned from seeing the neurologist, Lesley once again shifted into high gear. She strongly felt I needed to escape the isolating and depressive energy of MacDougall and avoid relocating to any place like it. She wanted to find a clean, peaceful, and healthy place for me to live, one where I could get help with daily tasks I now found difficult or impossible to handle on my own, things like cooking, cleaning, and showering. Once, I found myself thinking that, in some ways, I'd been more of a man as a child.

Friends and family thought it was time I escaped the isolation and dark energy of the MacDougall House too. No one felt more strongly about it than Lesley. She called an acquaintance who worked with the handicapped and asked him to recommend a place nearby that might suit a person with physical challenges like mine. He immediately suggested an assisted living complex in the Berkshire Hills of New York. It stood about half an hour from Lesley's door.

When Lesley paid her daily visit to me that night at the rehab center, she sat down with me on the sofa in my room.

"Wouldn't it be great if we lived closer to each other?" she asked, knowing my answer would be the same as hers. It got me thinking. What if moving to that place would stop me from worrying about Lesley growing tired of doing so much for me.

"This could be a great place for you," she said. "You're always doing ridiculous things like driving into the snow in your wheelchair in the middle of the night. You were going wind up in a ditch or something."

"First of all, I've never gone out in the middle of the night. Secondly, I wasn't going to sleep in a ditch. I don't even like sleeping in them all that much."

"You just do crazy things sometimes!" she said, shaking her head at me.

"I'm sorry, but to me, some things carry a foul smell. 'Assisted living' for instance. If it applies to me, at least." I always winced at the idea of being shoved to the end of the platform before I was good and ready to go.

"I looked at this place on its website," Lesley said brightly. "It looks lovely!"

I glanced at her in silence. "I just don't see myself living in a place like that!" I said stoically. "How old do you think I am? What, am I your grandfather?"

"I don't have a grandfather."

"If you *did* have one, do you think he would look anything like me?"

"You're not an old man. Not yet," she teased me.

"Right. And I might never get there." Lesley didn't say anything. I slowly started considering the prospect. "So, how does it work in a place like that?" I said. "What, they make your meals, tuck you at night?"

"Oh, come on!" she replied. "I doubt it's like that at all."

I got quiet for a few seconds. "Couldn't I just buy a new body?" I asked her. Lesley didn't respond. I thought I must have made her sad. "OK," I said. "What am I looking at here? I can't really live alone anymore. And I can't expect you to spend all your time taking care of me. So, what—is this kind of place all that's left for me?"

"Oh, believe me, there are way worse places you could wind up," Lesley assured me. "If you were to live in *this* place," she went on, "your stress would go way down. And we both know stress isn't good for any disease, including yours."

"Actually, I think disease sees stress as a real help," I said.

"Anyway, what about the stress of living in a place where every person has one foot out the door?"

"Don't we all?" asked Lesley.

"I suppose so," I said. "But living in a place like that would forever be pushing that in my face."

"In some ways, that's a good thing, don't you think?" she said.

A few days later, Lesley folded up my wheelchair, put it in the car and we drove into New York state to have a look at the place called Camphill. It sat about half an hour from Lesley's house, just over the Massachusetts border. We drove through the downtown of a quiet little hamlet called Chatham, the same name as the New Jersey town where my mother lived after she and my father divorced. We cruised up a two-lane road and found our way to the entrance. Pulling in the driveway, we passed a small sign on a post in the grass: ELDERS IN COMMUNITY. I quickly revised it in my mind, ELDERS IN CAPTIVITY. I would be in my fifties for another year, and I wanted to remain there indefinitely.

Lesley and I started a slow, winding drive up the hill, peering out the windows at the trees and flowers and attractive wooden buildings marking our way. Being surrounded by low hills of green grass gave me a frail hope that this place might offer me some minor salvation. We continued touring the grounds, and though I was trying to cast everything in the brightest light possible, the scenes we passed through felt like a graveyard. Then I saw the first waves of white. A great many of the elders walking along the road sported white hair. Suddenly, the feeling of life gave way to the color of snow and bone.

I glanced at Lesley in silence. "No way I'm moving here," I told her, defiantly. She rolled her eyes.

We drove up the drive and stopped against the curb at the end of a long sidewalk that led to the main building. Lesley turned the car toward a parking space with a 'handicap' sign. "Great!" she said. "How convenient! Right next to the front door."

I saw nothing comforting about discovering an available parking space close to the entrance of my final stop in this world. Taking in the blue sign with its picture of a wheelchair silenced me for a moment, the span of a breath. Though the place screamed old age and death, I had begun to worry that needing a wheelchair would disqualify me as a resident. But I remembered Lesley telling me about her phone call with the head administrator, in charge of meeting prospective residents and introducing them to the place. As the woman had explained to Lesley, in order for me to qualify for living there, I simply had to be able to transfer into the bed unaided. She said I would get help with dressing and showering and other simple but essential tasks of daily life and would get three nutritious, often home-grown organic meals a day. I reminded myself that by living there, I would never again lie on a bathroom floor alone, trying to figure out how to get up.

We continued down the hall toward her office. With Lesley walking beside me, I glanced at the exhibit of watercolors on the wall, bitterly resenting having to be here, hating the idea that I might be moving somewhere only because it offered the kind of help I didn't think I would ever need.

Lesley and I stood at the open office door. A handsome, friendly-looking woman sat behind a large, wooden desk and looked up.

"Sean? Lesley?" she said in a friendly voice. "Pease come in." She stood and motioned to the chairs in front of her desk.

"Have a seat." I was already seated. Lesley sat down. "How was your trip? Did you have any trouble finding us?"

"No, no trouble at all," Lesley answered. I just smiled. I didn't know what else to do.

The woman beamed at us. "We've been expecting you," she said, looking directly at me. I knew she meant not just about the appointment but on some kind of deeper level.

It stunned me. *Who* had been expecting me? And why, in God's name? I wasn't supposed to be there. The whole thing felt terribly wrong. Ludicrous. I smiled grimly at this stranger; it was important to me that she remain one. It almost felt like a matter of life and death. No one coveted my life, but it was mine. I wanted it back. A shield had lowered itself in my brain and muffled everything, even my thoughts.

The three of us talked for half an hour, though I mostly listened. I refused to believe that I belonged in this place. A mistake had obviously been made. A bad one. No doubt it would soon be rectified somehow. I simply had to play my part and not look like the least threat to anyone. I knew the lines I had to mouth, and I silently began gathering my forces for the soon-to-be-coming escape. I wouldn't bother thinking about where I could go and how I might get there; leaving the details of it all vague seemed the best course. It appeared that my moving there was a done deal. The only question was whether my life was, too.

After our meeting, Lesley and I left the building, to my great relief. I just wanted to make tracks as rapidly as possible out of what I thought of as 'the compound.' I had never felt more at risk of eternal imprisonment.

"Do you want to take a spin around the place" Lesley asked me. "It would give you a better sense of it."

"I'd rather not," I told her. "Can we just head back to town? Why don't we have lunch at the Indian place?"

"We will," said Lesley with a smile. "But let's just check out the grounds. They're really beautiful." I didn't want to push it. Lesley had found a place for me that she must have thought would be a huge improvement over the place I'd been calling home since she'd met me.

"OK," I said. "But let's not take too long. I'm kind of tired."

Lesley led us down the walk that circled the building. To our right sat a large green field. Toward its center stood a small wooden gazebo topped by an upright metal post with a weather vane attached. A rooster perched on a slender arrow above the steeple's tip and was turning this way and that in a gentle wind. I didn't want to admit it, but my surroundings resembled a sanctuary of sorts, home to flowers and trees and the softening songs of birds. Over my head hung a pastel blue sky being crossed by pure white clouds. For a moment, I abandoned my defiant stance toward the place. I'd left many homes over the years, and I stubbornly resisted thinking I'd found another. It would be a long time before I knew I had.

CHAPTER 17

Life In The Slow Lane

After a week at Camphill, my mood hadn't shifted, and I began to worry. Every once-in-a-while in my life, I've felt down for several hours, even for a day, but by the following morning, I had always snapped out of it, sometimes even forgetting about the whole thing. But not this time. In the dining room, I sat with people from other generations who out-distanced me by two or three, even four decades. I was fifty-nine when I moved in; Florence had just turned ninety-eight. It was obvious I'd taken a wrong turn.

Every morning before breakfast, the residents (I thought of them as inmates) reported to the office, where medications were passed out, ointments spread, vitamin-rich drinks swallowed, etc. And it seemed I was one of them! Soon, I'd be taking more than ten pills before beginning my day. A few of the residents muttered quietly to themselves; some made no apparent sense at all when they carried on conversations, sometimes with an invisible friend. A couple of individuals never spoke at all. One evening, I was walking down the hall to the refuge of my room when the elderly woman, who used to live in #58, where I lived now, emerged from my doorway wearing my baseball cap and carrying a book of mine under her arm. One woman drooled down her chin and onto the front of her shirt; an eighty-five year old man sometimes quoted the Bible to anyone who would listen. I had begun living in a quiet panic over the idea I might never being released from this penitentiary. I felt better when I told myself, and believed it, that I wouldn't be living here very long. But I would eventually appreciate that a fantasy life can be very hard to escape. One man sat for hours in his room carrying on a conversation with a friend who never poked his head out the door or spoke loudly enough for me to hear him. It would be some time before I realized the friend didn't exist. Another talked endlessly about how he'd be going home to Chicago soon. That day, of course, would never arrive.

    I was never quite sure what it meant to be at my wit's end, but at my new home I was finding out. I had been trying for a couple of weeks to feel happy, or at least on my way back, but I kept falling short of the mark. It seemed clear a change of perspective was needed. On my second week there, I rolled down the hall on my way to the med room to get my morning pills. I came to the little blackboard outside the dining hall and scanned it to see what I'd be missing if I stayed in my room yet again. Beneath the reminders of Bingo and storybook hour appeared the notice for the poetry group, led by a man named John. Was he a retired bank manager or someone looking to be of service to his community? I grimly imagined finding senile elders sitting around a table reading poems by Henry Wadsworth Longfellow or Poe or others whose verses I'd read in high school. I discovered that the group met every Thursday from eleven till noon in the library. I felt excited, not having thought there would be a library in the building, let alone an hour each week when people read poetry together. I stopped at the med room to get my pills and ask a question of whomever was on duty that morning. I pulled up to the wall across from the office and waited my turn for supplements.

    In ten minutes, Katharina, one of the home health aides (HHAs) ushered me into the room. I wheeled up to the sliding table, and Katharina slid open the drawers on the medicine cart one at a time. She started selecting small bottles and singly taking out pills, placing them into a tiny paper cup. I watched her work, this middle-aged woman with a ready smile, who seemed calm and friendly and extremely patient. She slid the pills into one of the cups and set it on the rolling table.

"Here you go," she said. "Down the hatch, or whatever you say."

"Those are for me?" I asked, smiling.

Yes," she said. "Your doctor wanted you to take them."

"All of them?" I asked. "Nice guy. Remind me to get a new doctor."

We laughed. She would quickly become one of my favorites on the staff. It seemed possible Katharina's presence would help me settle down, even feel a little at home.

I'd never wanted to wind up at my age in a situation like this. I didn't exactly feel lucky to be here, but I clearly needed to live in a place like this, and I had a strong suspicion there weren't many facilities remotely like it. I had heard horror stories about paying extended visits to other long-term care facilities.

"What do you know about the poetry group?" I asked Katharina. "I'm thinking of checking it out. Who's John, the guy leading it?"

"He's one of the people who work here," she said. "He does a lot of things. He works in the garden, gives talks, helps run different ceremonies. And he's a writer. He's written two or three books of poems in German. And another one or two in English. I've heard the poetry group is excellent. You might like it." And she went no further.

Camphill is possibly the only facility in the world designed to serve both the elderly and people with 'special needs,' all of whom are developmentally disabled.

Katharina is one of about twenty Home Health Aides who work at Camphill, many of whom I would get to know well and implicitly trust. They are forever on the move, traveling from one place to another—residents' rooms, the dining hall—wherever they're needed. They carry out their long list of duties, regularly assisting people with tasks they once had no trouble doing on their own. I hate to think I make their highly demanding jobs harder, but I'm able to consistently succeed at doing just that. I often lose my temper when my computer is malfunctioning or when I think someone has needlessly relocated something in my room. I always get angry at my body's reluctance to do the simplest things I ask of it, such as buttoning my shirt or transferring unaided onto the shower bench. The aides—almost all of them women—are far from sufficiently thanked. They regularly see people at their worst (me very much included), and they perform their wide-ranging duties with an efficiency and grace I can only admire. In time I would come to regard them as angels of mercy in the flesh, often making me feel I have arrived someplace strongly resembling heaven, one where clouds are filled not with rain but laughter and the best of good will.

After breakfast, I wheeled down the hall. After passing the dining room, I turned into the corridor connecting the two sides of the building. In half a minute, I had rolled to the other side of the building looking for the library. I didn't know exactly where I was headed, or if I should bother to go. For many years, I'd taught poetry in a high school for the performing arts. The students wrote poetry every day. They loved putting on paper things they needed to say, though not always out loud. At times, I couldn't relate to what they'd written, but very often their words set off sparks in me. They brought me places I didn't expect to go, and I felt indebted to them for that. Spending time with them often left me feeling younger and more alive. What could these ancient specimens bring me, I wondered, like the snob I was, a certified, unapologetic ageist. Though I would never have agreed, I deserved to feel ashamed of myself, especially as I was walking the same road as these people, who were several turnings ahead of me, and whose minds were far more open than mine.

I pushed open the door to the library fully expecting to be underwhelmed by what I was about to see. What I found, instead, were nine or ten people sitting around a wooden table looking very happy to be there. Right away, I realized I had some catching up to do. I was ready to wheel up to the table, but there was no space for my wheelchair. A woman quickly got up and made room for me, waving me forward. "Come right in here," she said to me with a smile. "We won't bite."

"Well, I won't" said a friendly man named Richard in a British accent. "I promise. I seriously doubt anyone else here will either." People laughed, good-humoredly.

"I've already had my breakfast," said a woman at the other end of the table with a chuckle. And so began my education.

When I crossed the library threshold that morning, I entered a world I hadn't expected to see, largely because I had never lived in a place like this. I had led a group in poetry writing at an elder hostel years before, but only for a couple of weeks one summer. I certainly hadn't wanted to relocate to living quarters such as those. Yet, I was slowly starting to think

I may have made that very move. I had always seen the people called seniors as being 'over the hill,' a geographic marker I believed, when I thought about it, would be forever out of *my* reach, a sort of mythic setting I never wanted to call home.

The woman who had graciously moved a few seats down to make room for me lay her book on the table in front of her. This was Dot. "I want to read one of the first poems I read by him. But first, I'll read something he said." Dot looked down and opened her notebook. "Your task is not to seek for love, but merely to seek and find all the barriers within yourself that you have built against it." I suddenly wondered what walls I had built between myself and my new home. I couldn't imagine coming to love living here. But the fruits of my imagination have often taken a long time to ripen.

Dot looked up and caught my eye. I saw light and life in those eyes. "This poem marks the beginning of a long, wonderful relationship with Rumi, the sender of incomparable poems, I as the ever-grateful receiver."

She began to read another poem, one I didn't recognize immediately. I was suddenly intrigued by these people.

'It so happens I am sick of being a man.

And it happens that I walk into tailor shops and movie
 houses

dried up, waterproof, like a swan made of felt

steering my way in a water of wombs and ashes.'

"When did Rumi live?" asked James, looking down the table at Richard. Everyone turned to Richard; they usually did when a question about the writer (or almost anything else, it seemed) needed answering. I would come to see that he ranked as an expert on subjects large (the existence of higher worlds) and small (the cultivation of buckthorn bushes). For a man of his talents and knowledge, Richard was innately modest.

"That was Neruda, not Rumi," Dot corrected.

"That's right. Rumi was from Persia," Richard concurred. "He was a Sufi mystic and lived in the 13th century. He couldn't have gone to movie houses." I laughed. Richard continued. "His poems have been translated into many languages. He's actually the best-selling poet in the world!"

I felt that I was back in college, and that I could learn interesting things in this place. I wouldn't be given homework here. But I wouldn't have cared; for the past several years, my mind had pretty much been on hold. A few years ago, my disease had firmly gotten the upper hand. I felt my mind had sunk into a dry place: nothing inspired me or kept me in touch with the deepest parts of myself. I felt empty and needed to be filled with new ideas and vistas. I wondered if that could possibly happen in a place that seemed to be keeping pace with a slowly diminishing pulse.

Richard asked Dot to read the Neruda poem again. After she read the poem a second time, the ten of us silently took in the words. I was delighted by the expressive way she recited it. I was vaguely familiar with the Chilean poet's work, and instantly decided to take out a volume of his poetry from the town library. (Normally about ten residents went there once a week on our shopping trip.) The poem Dot read had moved me. I hadn't thought that would happen here. For a few weeks, all I could think of was how long I'd have to bide my time in this place before I moved out and re-entered my actual life. (It was still to be a little time before I realized the life I knew was gone.)

The second week the group met, I read a poem I had written years ago when I taught poetry in the charter high school. The world I knew back then stood in sharp contrast to where I found myself today, but the two contained very similar light and shadows. I call the poem 'Therefore,' and though it was written for a very different audience, I felt sure some members of this one would be familiar with the terrain, even if they'd never walked it themselves.

Therefore

I think
therefore I am
unhappy.

I hope
therefore I am
still here.

The doors in front of which I had been so morosely standing were slowly opening for me. I started going to poetry every week and feeling I was back in a setting where I felt at home, a feeling I thought I'd never have again. I began to write poems once more, something I hadn't done since I started making the rounds of rehabilitation clinics. Listening to Dot read Neruda that day forced me to dismount my high horse and accept that people of any age could share good poems, theirs and those by other people, and talk insightfully about it all.

And so, I began writing in earnest. The group got me back on my feet, figuratively, and Richard was an important part of it, reading his lovely poems and talking brilliantly about poetry and the craft of writing it. I embarked on writing my memoir and started looking for a good place to work. I tried the café across from the dining hall, a room on the other side of the building, where the independent residents lived. I even tried writing in my own room. None of the places felt right, so I tried one more, a room down the hall just a few doors down from my bedroom. It overlooked flowering bushes inside a ten-foot wooden fence of attractively weathered boards. On the other side of the fence was a tall row of red maple trees and behind them was the sky. The room's windows stretched from the floor almost to the ceiling, letting me see the earth, the boughs of the trees, and the heavens. I instantly knew I had found a sanctuary, one filled with light, which has always been my seat of inspiration. I hadn't seen a window like it in a very long time. I finally began to feel glad to have moved into a place I hadn't wanted to believe I had reached. My illness has taken from me many things I treasured and never thought I'd have to live without. I would quickly come to treasure this room with all its light and the crowns of green trees. Even curtains on the windows would change the space, make it smaller, less spiritually-centered and alive. I was confident that in this room I should always feel inspired.

Dot, a painter, was one person I was sure appreciated the transcendent power of light. She often came to this room to create her warm and inviting watercolors. After several weeks of sharing a table in the room where the poetry group met, Dot and I started drawing closer together. We sat at the same table in the dining room for every meal and found we had a great deal to say to each other. I never tired of listening to her and hoped she felt the same way about me. When we talked, Dot often wore a quiet smile. In time, I would carry a shadowed smile of my own. I sometimes imagined what might have happened had we been about the same age. I might not have asked her to marry me, but I would have thought about it.

Dot told me she had never written a poem. I found that unfortunate, both for everyone who could have read her words and for Dot herself. But she read a fair amount of poetry; Wordsworth, Robert Frost, Mary Oliver, and others. Richard and I began encouraging her to write poems of her own.

Like great painters, she saw beauty and uniqueness in every corner of the world around us and within us. When she finally graced us with a poem, I was overjoyed. "I'm so glad you've decided to write a poem," I said. "It was you who said life doesn't last forever."

"I *could* be wrong about that," she said with a smile, "but I kind of doubt it."

"I hope I didn't annoy you and put too much pressure on you."

She just smiled. There were plenty of people in the world I wouldn't have minded annoying. Dot wasn't among them. I didn't know quite what to make of her. Had we known each other before? I've always believed in reincarnation of some sort. How could I not, having grown up in a haunted house? Sometimes, I wonder if Dot and I had already spent a lot of time together. I could imagine Dot as my mother, sister, even my wife. Whatever our connection to each other might once have been, we seemed to be headed toward a deep friendship in this one.

"I didn't tell anybody, because I thought I couldn't do it, but I've always wanted to write a poem. I can cross that off my bucket list. Only a few dozen to go!"

I thought about it for a moment. If I'd *had* a bucket list, I would have moved seeing Dot every day near the top. And I could hardly have been in a better position to make it happen. All I had to do was walk to the end of a short hallway and turn the corner.

"So, Dot, do you mean to say you've never wanted to live in a garret, writing poetry and starving?"

"I can't say I have," she answered. "Sorry. It simply isn't on the list. There are so many places I want to see. Do you think less of me?"

"I very much doubt that could ever happen," I said.

"Don't be too sure," Dot said. "'Never' isn't the most reliable word. It's a noble fantasy, though."

I looked at her for a moment. Suddenly, a question occurred to me. "Dot, if you could live one day of your life again, what day would it be?"

She answered immediately, "Tomorrow." It stopped me. I wanted her to be around for a whole lot of them. At ninety-two, she wasn't young in the usual sense of the word. But she was vibrant, forward-looking, wide-eyed. And she took in as much of the world as she could. Dot helped me to believe the door to our life remains open unless we allow it to swing shut.

As the end approached for Dot, I could see and hear a subtle difference in the way she looked and carried herself. Her sparkling blue eyes didn't shine as brightly, her voice seemed a little muted and tired. At lunch one day, I asked her if I could stop by her room that afternoon. I feared she might not have many afternoons left.

"I was going to insist you do," she said warmly.

That she would have insisted on it worried me. A couple

of hours later, I was knocking on her door, as I'd done so many times.

"Dot?" I called out.

"Come on in," she said in a friendly tone.

I pushed back the door and wheeled in. She was lying in her bed smiling at me. "A new poem," I said, holding up the typed page. Dot sat up a little and took it. As she almost always did, she read the poem at once and read it again. Then she removed her glasses and looked at me. "That's lovely," she said. "Can I keep it?"

"Of course," I answered. "Just don't try to sell it."

Dot smiled and turned to the window. "There was a gold finch out here yesterday," she said. "When one of them flies by, it's hard to be sad about anything."

I decided I could have used a gold finch flying by right then. Or a flock of them.

After we talked for a little while, Dot looked out the window again. "I hope you don't mind," she said, "but I need to rest a little more. Go and write some more wonderful poetry."

"I certainly have time for it here," I said. "So do you. I'm still waiting for that poem you promised me about your father. I know you don't consider yourself a poet, but I'm afraid I can't agree. You've already written two great poems. It's time they had some company. High time."

"I hope you're a patient person," Dot said, chuckling.

"About some things," I said, looking her in the eye. "For some things to happen, I'd prefer to wait a long time."

Back in my room a few minutes later, I sat in front of the window and looked out. I was hoping to spot a gold finch. I had a hunch I thought I might be looking a long time.

Train

Your train used to run on these tracks.
I could hear the wheels rolling;
the sound made me feel
that all was well with the world.
The birds flew past your window,
asking you to paint their sky
and let them carry your dreams aloft.
The evidence of my loving you
is stamped indelibly on my heart.
You're sailing through amber now
and haven't really left me.
I live a short walk from your door
close to memories of a strong, gently winding current,
and I smile when I think of you
and feel the breath of joyful tears,
letting your echo seep deeply into me
as a curl of gold-colored cloud.
You gave me countless measures of a melody
I shall always hear and miss forever.

Every Friday afternoon we went shopping. The van took up to fifteen of us downtown, making all the usual stops: the bank, drugstore, library, health food store, and the supermarket. Everyone but me sat in ordinary seats, though getting in and out of the van proved challenging for some of us. Perhaps me more than anyone else in the van. I sat in my wheelchair in the back, behind everyone else. The van was equipped with four-person rows and had an aisle running down the middle. A few of the seats were usually vacant. I was not part of any conversation, mostly because everyone else had some degrees of hearing loss. My chair was held securely in place by straps on all sides, so my normal frustration at being unable to move as I wanted was a little more pronounced; it left me feeling pinned down, like a child or a prisoner, both of which categories I sometimes feel I belonged to. But I felt positively joyous the moment the van pulled out from the grounds of Camphill and I breathed the air of freedom. The usual driver of the van was an eminently likeable man named Nick, a local tour guide, philosopher, and comedian. He's taken me to countless medical appointments and often made me feel the ride wasn't long enough.

Every week, my favorite stop of all, the one most deeply tied to my emotional equilibrium, was the library. To me, libraries are bastions of sanity and critical knowledge of the human spirit. More than any place I know, the library feels like a refuge, even a church, a peaceful harbor where I never feel pressured or rushed and can enjoy relative silence, something in short supply in our busy world. Something I treasured at this library was the presence of a twenty-eight year-old poet, writer of short stories and memoirs, a librarian in training: she made me glad to be in her company for half an hour every Friday. We are separated by decades, and because of that and her love of the written word, she reminded me strongly of the students I used to have. We regularly exchanged bits of our writing, and I've saved almost every word. And like those other students, Carly taught me easily as much as I taught her. She helped resurrect those figures inside the shadows, memories of a world that has become increasingly difficult to bring into focus.

Our last stop on the junket was the supermarket. Nick brought us to the front door and everyone stepped off in a kind of slow, fitful ballet. No one moved quickly, but everyone moved more easily than I did. After Nick got me to the parking lot, I rolled through the foyer, leaning over to snatch a plastic hand cart as I passed. I began wending my way up and down the aisles, scanning the shelves for items I might want. I once asked Nick what he thought of the supermarket. "I'm not crazy about it, but what am I going to do?" he asked. "I'm not Daniel Boone. I'm not going to hunt my own meat. I don't even wear a coonskin cap!" I laughed and waited to see if there were more. With Nick, there usually was. "You know what Oscar Wilde said: 'Be yourself. Everyone else is taken.'"

Turning down one of the aisles, the music floating down from the ceiling speakers suddenly stopped me in my tracks. For a couple of days, I had been trying to recall the name of a favorite rock band of mine and always came up short. I hadn't listened to the band in years, but my love for them hadn't faded. Suddenly my favorite song of theirs was wafting through the air from the speakers in the ceiling. I needed to immediately mark down the name of the song. I refused to be dependent any longer on a memory that had obviously seen better days. I was only in my early sixties, but I suddenly thought it possible I had begun that unstoppable slide down the brittle edge of dementia. I now lived with an older population, and thoughts of mental deterioration were anchored uncomfortably in my brain.

I went directly to the deli counter and asked the attendant if I could borrow a pen and piece of paper to write down a few words. The friendly woman gave them to me. I laid the paper on the counter and quickly wrote down 'Gin Blossoms.' I ordered a slice of pizza and a soda, possibly, unconsciously, because it seemed like a meal more common among the young than people worrying about getting dementia and perhaps already experiencing its onset.

I folded the paper and slid it into my pocket. Then rolled over to a table and set down my lunch. After taking a few bites of the pizza, I reached into my pocket to make sure the paper was still there. It was. I pulled it out and opened it. 'Gin Blossoms' stared back at me and I took a breath. I started calling up other memory losses I had suffered recently and wondering what it might mean to have started piling them up. Predictably, my stubborn hypochondriac instantly dusted off the names of potential candidates, including my prize culprit: brain tumor. I shook my head at the idea and smiled a little grimly. I once believed that having a real disease had relieved my overworked imagination of one of its more onerous occupations, sniffing out the scent of oncoming disaster. Suddenly I saw that my imagination, with its penchant for spoiling any party organized by delusional thinking, was still very much on duty.

I started considering how much my ongoing health struggles—along with the stress of having resettled somewhere I thought still years away for me—was probably compromising my brain cells, making it hard for them to hold onto all the components of my new life. This thinking calmed me considerably. I realized that being a hypochondriac was a voluntarily acquired distinction and something I could readily discard.

A minute later, I was retracing my route to the store's front doors, keeping the jam-packed hand cart centered on my lap. I looked over the pile of items I was bringing home and made sure I hadn't forgotten anything. For a few minutes, I lazily watched other shoppers entering or leaving the building, and looked around to spot Nick on his way back. Suddenly, I realized with horror that I might not have paid for my groceries. I couldn't remember having done it, and there didn't seem to be a receipt anywhere in sight. Just then, Beverly and Claire, both in their eighties, pushed their loaded shopping carts to my wheelchair, looked at me and smiled. "Get everything you needed?" Beverly asked me with a smile. "I'm sure Nick won't be here for a few minutes, so if you forgot something we'll still be here when you get back. So, if there's something you need, go back in and grab it."

I thought for a moment. "Do you think this place stocks brain cells?" I joked. "Mine don't seem to be up to snuff."

"God!" said Claire, chuckling. "I haven't heard that expression in an aeon." She paused. "What *is* an aeon, anyway?" she asked.

"My father used to use that expression, all the time," Beverly said. "Drove my mother nuts! I think she almost left him for it."

"Boy, I can remember—*barely*," said Claire, smiling at me. "I can remember when I was a kid, and getting older was something I looked forward to. I thought it would make people take me seriously. Now, I'm an old lady, and nobody takes me seriously."

"No offense, ladies," I said, smiling, "but I'm not looking forward to getting older. I keep looking for a detour."

"Hey, if you find it, let us know!" said Beverly.

"Definitely," Claire chimed in. "I'll even drive."

"Oh no, you won't," Barbara said. "At your age, you couldn't be a safe driver."

"Look who's talking," Claire retorted.

"Ladies, please!" I smiled. "Act your age!" All three of us laughed.

*

Brian and Anna's small, comfortable house sat just down the road from the main building, where I lived. Their front yard was full of flowers: bleeding hearts, sunflowers, wisteria, morning glories, and many others. We began spending time together, often in their home. Anna put together wonderful, mostly vegetarian meals that usually featured a delicious soup, whole grain bread, cheese, green olives, and salads. The ever-expanding list of dinner guests included Camphill residents, together with friends and family, including Brian's sister and a friend of theirs who had once been a prominent member of the Manhattan publishing world. After dinner, the night was given over to music and poetry. Anna would play Mozart on the piano and sometimes played the lyre, their son played the cello, I usually read a few of my poems, or had Brian read them in his lovely British accent. Once, a young German volunteer at Camphill played a fairly complex original piano composition entirely from memory. A few times, Lesley came to dinner, carrying a Tangleberry pie.

It seemed Brian and Anna put wellness at the apex of the qualities they believed central to happiness. They saw wellness of the mind and spirit as more important than that of the body. I believe they saw physical health as wonderful but not necessary to be one with the sacred. They weren't overly interested in physical affliction in itself, mine or anyone's. They didn't see disease as a separate playing field on which the worth of a life, or of one's being, could be accurately measured. I'm fairly sure they believed the most important story is of how one responds to difficulties, with an eye on the well-being of the soul.

Brian and Anna were always buoyant and comforting, holding a seemingly unshakeable faith that the world was heading (even if very slowly sometimes) in an ultimately positive direction. It wasn't as though they couldn't see the troubles revolving around each of us on our journey, they just refused to see them as end points. Brian and Anna made up my favorite married couple and were an unfailing inspiration to would-be lovers like me, a testament to the often unspoken— but impossible to ignore—currents of love winding its way through the world. They were parents and grandparents but still children in the most precious sense of the word.

"Can I tell you about the dream I had during my operation?" I asked them, a few days after the emergency surgery I'd had that year to clear a life-threatening blockage in my colon. One morning I'd woken up at Camphill with my abdomen so bloated I looked positively pregnant. Before I was taken to the operating room, the surgeon took Lesley aside and told her that if he didn't perform the surgery, I would die.

"I'm not even sure it was dream," I told them, "but here's what I saw: a line of people were standing against two of the walls of the operating room looking at me. I'd never seen any of them before. Who were they? Just the product of the anesthesia? But they stared kindly at me, and I wasn't scared of them at all."

"They were angels," Anna replied at once.

"You really think so?" I said, skeptical. "Angels?"

"They're always there," said Brian calmly. "They'll always *be* there."

"It's not an uncommon vision when people are on the verge of crossing over," said Anna flatly.

There may well be invisible entities watching over us. I've often wondered about such things, but it could well be wishful thinking on my part. Marty, one of my best friends for many years, would undoubtedly think it was, but he is unwilling to believe in a hidden realm, unless we're talking about things such as emotions, ideas, or the laws of physics. I would like to believe there's magic in the world, I just don't want my desires to make a fool of me. Brain and Anna would doubtlessly tell me there's only one person who can make a fool of me: I know him personally, and he's hardly an angel. And who knows, maybe those angels saved my life.

One day, Greta, one of the activities directors, asked me if I'd like to work with a couple of the special needs residents on their poems. "Judy and Gail love to write poetry," Greta told me. "They'd be excited to sit down with you, especially because you write poetry. What do you say?"

"It sounds like fun," I answered. "I really miss teaching."

"It sounds like a good deal for everyone!"

"It does," I said. "I do have one question, though."

"Sure," Greta said. "What's your question?"

"Well, I just need to know what it pays. You know, I made serious money when I taught high school English!" For a moment, I was afraid she'd think I was serious, but she quickly started to grin.

I hadn't spent too much with Judy and Gail. I was never quite sure how to react to them. Judy regularly carried on running conversations with herself; often beginning by addressing someone, but she isn't slowed down if the person pays her little or no attention. Gail often sulked and could get highly irritated if you unwisely ask her a question when she's busy wallowing in whatever it happens to be. But both Gail and Judy loved writing poems, and it mattered that others pay attention to what they wrote with me.

I would come to see that these 'special needs' people were not all that different from the rest of us in most ways. Yes, they followed their own drummers, and until one learned the key signature they worked from, it was easy to feel left behind. At first, I heard the rhythms as irregular ones at best, and the conductor normally kept to the shadows. But, it seemed to me that everyone has his or her own special needs. Of course, that generally refers to intellectual or emotional difficulties rather than physical ones. Not too long ago, people with my sort of challenges were called 'cripples.' I sometimes wonder if it's the designation we object to or just having the condition it refers to.

I've never been a fan of labeling people, a practice that leaves as much out of the picture as it includes. A 'special needs' neighbor of Judy's at another Camphill in the state had a father who played first cello in the New York Philharmonic. One day, they were riding in the car together listening to a symphony on the radio.

"Listen to the bassoon here," said his father. "Just beautiful!"

Danny listened for a few seconds and responded without taking his eyes off the road. "Oboe."

"No, that's the bassoon," his father corrected him. "Isn't it glorious?"

"Oboe," Danny repeated. To his father's astonishment, after further listening to the symphony, he realized his special needs son was right.

I would sit down with Judy and Gail on separate days in

'my office,' the room where I did almost all of my own writing. We faced each other across the table, and I would take out a notebook and a pen. I normally began by asking them what they wanted to write about. If they didn't come up with anything, I would make a suggestion.

Judy loved animals. She often sat on her bed and followed the movements of the birds and rabbits and squirrels. Once, she saw a chipmunk scurrying across the lawn outside her window.

Chipmunks

Chipmunks aren't monks,
and they don't eat potato chips;
they sleep underground
with the bees and the rabbits
and whatever else dozes down there.
Chipmunks love nuts;
but they don't eat peanut butter.
I've never seen one ride a bicycle or fly a kite,
or push a wheelbarrow.
They don't swim,
though dogs do,
and raccoons, and once in a while, even cats.
But chipmunks do one thing quite well:
they look cute and make me smile.
What more could I ask of them,

or anyone else.
I'm not greedy,
and I know a gift when I see one.

She was very philosophical about growing older and didn't seem to mind the idea.

My Hair

In the morning my hair sticks straight up:
someone needs to brush it down,
and that's usually me.
I doubt hair likes to be brushed,
But I don't really like to brush it.
My hair was black when I was a kid,
and I want it to stay that way forever.
It might turn white as snow,
and I'll like it just fine.
If my hair goes white,
I can hide in the clouds,
say hello to the birds,
and hear the thunder up close.

Gail loved animals just as much as Judy did.

Cardinal

Today the trees have no leaves;
all the branches are bare,
and the wind is having its way.
But soon spring will drive off winter's white
and green will inherit the world.
A few months ago,
I saw a cardinal outside my window
I sat on my chair
and watched him fly off
I don't know where he went
I might have asked him as he was leaving,
but he wouldn't have heard me.
And, anyway,
birds don't talk;
they have better things to do.

Like Judy, Gail was forever captivated by the natural world and loved how it welcomed her on every side.

Painting A Watercolor

I painted a watercolor today;
I'll let it dry overnight
And look at it again tomorrow,
The teacher put it away after class.

I don't know where,
but I know I will see it again when it's dry.
I used different paints:
Sky yellow
Sunset orange
And a purple like rhubarb.
I like pretty colors,
But not on my fingers.
I have a hard time getting the paint off my skin,
I'll never get paint off my mind.

    It seemed Judy and Gail were always eager to sit down at the table with me and work on their poems; and that made me happy. I often wondered what colors Judy and Gail see when we write poems together, whether they're writing about a flower, an animal, a place, or someone that means a lot to them; the colors they called up were always brighter than those in my own poems. I quickly came to feel that Judy and Gail were doing me a favor as large as the one I hoped I was doing for them. They taught me, among other things, that poetry, both writing it and reading it, can be fun. For me, writing poems with them provided a fine lesson in gratitude, something I've struggled with since I felt my body shutting doors in me. Tracy once told me she believed Camphill had saved my life. When she said it, I thought she didn't understand all I had lost over the years, or that I felt the world had decided against giving anything back. When I think about writing poems with Judy and Gail, I realize life has been giving something back to me. I have a hard time coming up with a better way to spend my days.

My brother and sisters visited me a few weeks after I moved in. They very much wanted to see my new home and take in the surrounding countryside. They toured the interior of the building and seemed favorably impressed with the cleanliness and bright space of the rooms.

"This is great!" Claudia said, smiling at me. "You so needed to move someplace like this."

"That place where you were living was close to a slum," said Christian, chuckling. "I feared for my life when the sun went down."

Tracy stood in front of the window, looking through upper branches of the trees with her painter's eye, gazing at the blue sky. "You are going to be so at peace here," she said. "That will be great for your health."

"Yeah, physical and mental," said Claudia.

"They're close to the same thing," said Christian.

In a little while, all three of them decided to head home. We made our way to the front door and stepped outside.

"Don't be a stranger!" I said, after we all hugged.

"I don't think I could *get* any stranger!" said Christian, chortling.

"It'd be hard," said Tracy. "But I have total faith in you." She punched him playfully on the shoulder, and my sisters started walking toward the car.

Christian was quietly looking at me. "Lesley found this place for me," I said. "That's the kind of thing she does."

"Don't ever lose her," he said.

"If I haven't lost her by now, I think I'm home free," I said. Christian wasn't listening. He was unusually quiet, looking around at the building in front of us and the green lawn lying around the gazebo. He looked at me and smiled. "I'm not going to worry about you anymore," he said softly. He smiled, grabbed his hat, then he turned and walked off. Somehow, I knew he *wouldn't* worry about me anymore. I'd never felt happier to have fallen through a crack in the world.

In April, I felt spring finally arrive, winter now only a memory, unpleasant but moving off like a fog. I began revisiting sights and sounds I had almost lost hope of ever meeting up with again. I wheeled around the Camphill grounds every day, weather permitting. I felt I could hardly have survived the conditions of a Berkshire winter in my current state, and as a result, I tended not to go out much, should the weather be even modestly inclement.

But, today was early April, and the sky was a gleaming blue waiting for me.

I wheeled down the path at the edge of the lawn and looked up. I sat straight in my chair on the lawn beside the gazebo. The sky hung like a curtain of ever-shifting light and shadow. Within patches of blue, the clouds spoke softly to me, swirling slowly in a never-ending, forever-changing parade of colors and shapes, tirelessly modifying themselves into unfailingly beautiful, surprising configurations. I could almost hear them if I listened closely enough. The heavens felt alive, clothed in an almost limitless palette of color and shape. Always different yet unfailingly and forever resplendent. The sky often seemed to be handing me the same challenge: find something more beautiful than me.

I certainly don't want to spend any more time in places such as MacDougall or the hospital lined with shining hallways and tragic tales. But there are many places I'd like to visit again:

the beach down the hill from Nanny's house in Greenport, its sand home to the wayward horseshoe crab; the leaf-strewn, autumn grass under the pin oak tree outside the window I looked out of as a boy, across the room from my brother's bed; the quiet banks of the Iowa River; the pond where I swam on lazy summer days when I didn't even know what it meant to worry; Lesley's large backyard, where dreams gathered and held me close. I've promised myself I will remember all the people who have etched a permanent place in my heart, people who are always infusing me with wonder and joy.

Today I try never to run the risk of walking into a wild storm and catching a chill. At one time in my life, I was susceptible to that kind of foolishness, but one day I thought it might be time I grew up. In hospitals, where I've spent far too much time, even though they were full of kind, loving people, there was never a mention, even an insinuation, of the soul. To me, hospitals seemed lifeless and cold and ruled by the rhythm of machines. Outside most hospital windows are parking lots full of cars in a landscape of concrete and steel. But the view I have now is home to flowers and trees and the softening songs of birds. Most of the people here are kind and loving, and they have the time to express it and allow me to be carried along in the current. I left home as a young man many years ago, and I feel I may have found another. I've made up my mind to keep out of the shadows, where the dark bird sings and the stars refuse to shine. I now see the tide need not drown me, the sandy floor is ever beneath my feet, and my body can learn to swim. I hope to keep my world filled with laughter and light. And I will always try to happily surrender to the terms of this world. The storm clouds have passed and life has begun to hum in my blood.

The End

Acknowledgments

Thank you to Jana, my editor, best friend, cheerleader and advocate, who never lets me give up on myself, and who pushed me harder than I would have liked, but took me to the finish line. Thanks to my sister Tracy, for her beautiful cover art, for being my one of my biggest fans and supporters throughout my life, and for always believing in me. Thank you to Claudia, my older and wiser sister, who has helped me in innumerable ways. Thank you to the staff and residents at Camphill Ghent, for giving me a place at the table, a loving home for eight years, and helping me to see things in new and wonderful ways. Thanks to Dan, Marty, Ani, Joe and John, friends and allies whose humor and friendship keeps me going in more ways than I can say. I am filled with gratitude for all of you.

Sean Vernon is a teacher, essayist, poet, singer/songwriter and composer who received his MFA from the Writer's Workshop at the University of Iowa. His writing has been featured in Smithsonian, Backpacker and Notre Dame magazines. His music can be found at the Emily Dickinson Homestead, on Spotify and Bandcamp. He co-authored the award-winning musical children's book, *Blanket of Stars*, with author Jana Laiz, as well a collection of original poems, *Configurations*, that offers us a glimpse into the inner workings of this accomplished artist. *All The Meadows Wide* is Sean's personal story of hope, humor and resilience in the wake of a devastating diagnosis.